FAILING OUR KIDS:
Why the Testing Craze Won't Fix Our Schools

Susan Lina Ruggles

Edited by
Kathy Swope and Barbara Miner

A Special Publication of Rethinking Schools, LTD.
Milwaukee, Wisconsin

Rethinking Schools, Ltd. is a nonprofit educational publisher of books, booklets, and a quarterly journal on school reform, with a focus on issues of equity and social justice.

To request additional copies of this book or a catalog of other publications, or to subscribe to the Rethinking Schools Journal, contact:

Rethinking Schools
1001 East Keefe Ave.
Milwaukee, Wisconsin 53212
(toll-free 1-800-669-4192)
www.rethinkingschools.org

Failing Our Kids: Why the Testing Craze Won't Fix Our Schools
        © 2000 Rethinking Schools, Ltd.

Cover photograph by Jean-Claude Lejeune.

Cover and book design by C.C. Krohne.
Layout by Word Working, Inc., Milwaukee, Wisconsin

Special thanks to the Rethinking Schools editorial board: Bill Bigelow; Linda Christensen; Beverly Cross; Brenda Harvey; Stan Karp; David Levine; Larry Miller; Bob Peterson; and Rita Tenorio.

Special thanks also to the Joyce Foundation of Chicago for their support of this project.

ISBN 0-942961-26-9

Library of Congress Card Number: 00-107602

Jean-Claude Lejeune

Standardized tests will never answer the question of what our children need to learn to be leaders and informed citizens in a multicultural, ever-changing world.

— *from the introduction to* Failing Our Kids

TABLE OF CONTENTS

The Testing Craze: An Overview

Parents and Students Talk Back

Views from the Classroom

TABLE OF CONTENTS

Standards, Testing, and Race

Alternatives to Standardized Testing

Policy and Background

Resources

FAILING OUR KIDS:
WHY THE TESTING CRAZE WON'T FIX OUR SCHOOLS

Jean-Claude Lejeune

The Testing Craze: An Overview

Failing Our Kids: An Introduction

BY KATHY SWOPE AND BARBARA MINER
On Behalf of the Rethinking Schools Editorial Board

"How is my child doing?" is the most frequent question a parent asks a teacher. "How are our schools doing?" is an equally common question asked by community members.

Both are important questions. Standardized tests, however, can't adequately answer them. Decades of experience and research show that mis-use of standardized tests distorts student learning, exacerbates inequities for low-income students and students of color, and undermines true accountability between schools, parents, and the community.

The problem goes beyond the growing obsession with test scores. The tests, often tied to state standards, can result in a narrowing of the curriculum and the imposition of a restricted, official view of what constitutes knowledge. In addition, standardized tests are often "high-stakes" measurements. This high-stakes approach mandates that students who fail a particular test be retained, denied access to a preferred high school, or, in some cases, even refused a high school diploma. Some districts and states also use standardized test scores to evaluate principals, teachers, and entire schools.

Most important, standardized tests will never answer the question of what our children need to learn to be leaders and informed citizens in a multicultural, ever-changing world.

Rethinking Schools is pleased to present this booklet, *Failing Our Kids: Why the Testing Craze Won't Fix Our Schools*, as a contribution to the movement against test-based reform. *Failing Our Kids* is not a comprehensive analysis but rather a sampling of key topics. Most of the readings are adapted from articles that appeared in *Rethinking Schools* and draw on the experience of parents, students, teachers, and activists from around the country.

Many of the political and corporate backers of standardized tests skillfully use the language of high standards to promote an agenda that, contrary to the rhetoric, will increase divisions between the haves and have-nots.

Some advocates of standardized testing hope to use tests to improve teaching standards in low-achieving schools. Clearly, some schools do not adequately serve their low-income students, students of color, students with special needs, and students who do not speak English as their first language.

The irony is that an inappropriate reliance on standardized tests is likely to make problems worse for such students.

African-American and Latino students, for example, are disproportionately failing "high-stakes" standardized tests. This has historical precedent. Dating back to the development of IQ tests at the turn of the century, standardized tests have been used to sort and rank children, most reprehensibly along racial and class lines, and to rationalize giving more privileges to the already privileged. Indeed the first standardized tests were developed to support theories of the intellectual superiority of northern European whites.

Given the historical use of standardized tests, it is little surprise that the latest testing craze coincides with a resurgence of the view of the intellectual inferiority of African-Americans, as seen in the 1995 publication of *The Bell Curve*; with a conservative upsurge that looks down on programs designed to counter institutionalized discrimination; and with a growing division between the rich and poor despite unprecedented economic prosperity.

Standardized tests do more than legitimize and preserve existing power relations. Standardized tests can shape teaching and learning in ways that can harm children. Teachers are increasingly pressured to drill students on the tests, even when

> *Mis-use of standardized tests can distort learning, exacerbate inequities, and undermine true accountability.*

J. Kirk Condyles / Impact Visuals

they know that the tests don't assess the most essential aspects of thinking and learning. Entire subject areas — such as music, art, social studies and foreign languages — are de-emphasized in some schools because they aren't tested. Students often internalize the judgments of the tests — as if test scores were the final word on one's knowledge or potential.

In addition, when standardized tests become the engine of reform, they narrow the discussion of what is truly needed to transform schools — improvements involving funding equity, class sizes, teacher training, and reducing child poverty.

Standardized tests also come packaged with demands for more standardized curriculum. These calls are part of a broader effort to promote a narrow version of what children should learn. As scholar and activist Harold Berlak notes in his essay on page 93, state-mandated standards and tests "are an effort to put an end to the most valuable asset of a multicultural society: its vibrant cacophony of views about what constitutes truth, knowledge, and learning, and about what young children ought and ought not to learn at school. Standardized curriculum and tests insist upon one set of answers, and only one."

Alternative Assessment

To acknowledge the origins and consequences of standardized tests is not, however, to dismiss parent and community concerns about how well our children are learning.

Developing more equitable forms of assess-

ment is essential to defeating calls for standardized curriculum and testing. Educators must acknowledge the need for schoolwide, district wide, or statewide assessment. Historically, social justice activists have used such aggregate data to show how schools fail to provide a quality education to all children — to highlight schools' "savage inequalities."

A significant section of *Failing Our Kids* outlines the potential benefits of "authentic assessments" or "performance assessments" — assessments that simulate real-life tasks and knowledge.

We want to sound some notes of caution on alternative assessments, however. New forms of assessment aren't inherently less biased than standardized tests; racist attitudes of educators can just as easily bias classroom observations or portfolio assessments. Moreover, new forms of assessment might simply be more effective ways of assessing a Eurocentric, low-level curriculum.

The challenge is two-fold. How can assessments help teachers to better know the strengths and weaknesses of their students' work — so that the teachers can help students to engage in thoughtful and complex work?

Second, how can assessments be used to nurture critical inquiry, problem-solving, and multiculturalism — so that students are better prepared to understand the world and change it?

The question, as is true with so many areas of school reform, is what will best foster more equitable schooling and promote skills and values that are necessary for a more just society. ❏

Standardized Tests: Common Questions

The following is based on an interview with Kathy Swope, an editor of Rethinking Schools *who taught for 20 years and is currently an administrator in the Division of Research and Assessment with the Milwaukee Public Schools. The interview provides a brief overview of issues further discussed in this book.*

Q. What is a standardized test?

Generally, people are referring to tests that are "standard" — they have the same questions, the same directions, the same time limits, the same answers — so that student scores can be compared. Standardized tests most often involve multiple-choice questions given to large numbers of students and scored by a computer which recognizes only one "correct" answer.

Q. What's wrong with standardized tests?

One big problem is that the tests generally permit only one correct answer. Therefore the tests penalize multiple perspectives. The tests also avoid questions that require a complicated, thoughtful answer. Because the tests are given under time constraints, they also privilege students who quickly come up with answers. In order to better sort students, the tests often have obscure or "trick" questions. Just two or three "wrong" answers can dramatically alter a score.

Many standardized tests are also norm-referenced. They are designed to compare, sort, and rank children. In a norm-referenced test, 50% of the children will always be "below average." They will fail, no matter what they do or know.

Standardized tests also have a long history of cultural bias. There have been attempts to eliminate bias, but the very structure, time limits, and types of thinking that are rewarded in standardized tests carry their own biases. There are many ways to process information and demonstrate one's intelligences. Standardized tests focus only on a limited range of standardized approaches and standardized answers.

Q. But some questions have only one right answer. The Declaration of Independence, for example, was signed in 1776, not in 1976.

Questions that only have one right answer tend to rely on rote memorization. They are fact driven instead of being driven by critical thinking and analysis, which reflect higher levels of learning. We don't want to encourage students to merely regurgitate isolated facts. We want students to learn facts and procedures as part of thinking deeply about issues, events, and people — and to also make connections and integrate what they know.

Q. If we don't have standardized tests, how do we know how our schools and children are doing?

There are other methods of assessment. One alternative is performance-based assessments. These ask children to perform actual tasks or create things that are of value in the real world — essays, research projects, science experiments, and so forth. A second alternative involves portfolios, which take a look at student work over a period of time. Many teachers encourage student projects, such as building models to scale, or role playing and skits, or science fairs, or writing short stories or essays. There are any number of ways that teachers can capture students' learning.

Q. But these assessments don't let parents know how their child's school is doing compared to schools in other neighborhoods, districts, or states.

If we as a society establish high expectations for all students, which would include reading, writing, critical thinking, and deep analysis, and we assess how students are doing along a continuum to meet those goals, we would know how our schools are doing. Just as all students are given standardized tests, all could be given more authentic types of assessments.

We should remember that the goal of assessment is, primarily, to help students learn and to provide them a quality education — not to constantly compare schools and students.

Finally, it is a myth that standarized tests are a good indicator of student progress. Standardized tests merely show how well a student is able to perform on a particular test, versus how well a student demonstrates in-depth understanding of a given subject — or the way a student actually constructs and uses knowledge.

Q. Are all standardized tests bad?

A. Some people would argue that, used in moderation, standardized tests are okay. However, the problem is not just with the standardized tests themselves, but also with how the tests are used. When the results are used to dictate what should be taught, when they are used to promote low-level thinking and memorization, when they are used to rank and track students, when they are used instead of more meaningful school reforms — these, in my mind, are educational disasters.

Q. Why do African–American and Latino students generally perform less well than Whites on standardized tests?

This is a complicated question and I will touch on a few points.

First, students of color sometimes receive fewer opportunties and a less rigorous education. This can be manifested in less-experienced teachers, a more remedial-type curriculum, larger classes and less individualized attention, lower expectations for students of color, and overall fewer resources in the school. Also, the parents' educational level is a strong indicator of how well a student will do on standardized tests. Due to the long history of discrimination and unequal opportunity, the families of many students of color have not had the economic and educational benefits of a higher education.

Second, there is cultural bias in standardized tests. This bias is not always overtly noticeable and sometimes is embedded in the very structure and design of the tests.

For example, an overt bias might involve the subject matter — is the question about yachts or famous white writers? But bias can also be embedded in the way language is used.

Use of language is fundamentally tied to cultural experience. The language of a standardized test ordinarily follows European, Anglo-Saxon

Jean-Claude Lejeune

language patterns. Further, standardized tests tend to reflect a linear mode of thinking. Yet the linear mode of thinking is not consistent with an Afrocentric world view and thinking style, which tends to be more eclectic and which reflects what can be described as a spiral pattern.

Q. The disparity in test scores can be used to argue for more resources for urban schools. Isn't that a good thing?

Can you give me one example where an urban school that had a large percentage of poor minority students received significant additional funding just because the school had low test scores? If so, then perhaps we can explore that as one reasonable use of standardized testing.

Q. People often refer to "high-stakes" testing. What do they mean?

Standardized tests are being used to make "high-stakes" judgments of students and, increasingly, schools. This is happening even though the test-makers themselves say the tests should never be the sole determinant of important educational decisions.

In essence, "high-stakes" means that, on the

basis of standardized test scores, students are being flunked, denied access to a desired course or school, or even denied a high school diploma. In addition, some schools or principals are being judged primarily on the basis of standardized test scores. Important educational indicators — attendance, grade point averages, dropout rates, the rigor of the curriculum — are downplayed or ignored.

Q. A standardized test doesn't take up that much time in a classroom. So why all the fuss?

Every minute of classroom time is valuable. Nothing should be taking place in a classroom that does not enhance teaching and learning.

In some cases, teachers spend an inordinate amount of time preparing for a standardized test — by practicing test-taking skills, teaching specifically to the test, and so forth.

In addition, the breadth of a curricular area cannot be captured on a standardized test. If teachers limit themselves to emphasizing what is on the standardized test, students are being cheated out of the richness of a rigorous, comprehensive curriculum.

Q. That sounds great if students are in a school with a rich curriculum. But what about schools where very little real learning goes on?

Some districts and administrators use standardized tests to ensure that students get a minimal level of education. But the level of education that we should be demanding for all students requires that we go way beyond what is inspired by standardized tests. My concern is that standardized tests are becoming the top bar of expectations, not the minimal bar.

Furthermore, if you rely on standardized tests to close the achievement gap, that's terribly misleading in terms of who will get a quality education. Students in more privileged groups will get not only the material on the standardized tests, but may also receive drama, art, music, and important elective courses. It's essential to under-

stand that relying on standardized tests has been shown to dumb-down the curriculum.

Q. Testing is everywhere in society and it's an important survival skill. What's wrong with teaching kids how to take standardized tests?

We have an opportunity — and a responsibility — to create a more just and more equitable world. We cannot do that if we continue to rely on the status quo in education and testing. Just as we have evolved technologically in the last quarter century, we need to evolve with our assessment practices.

QUOTABLE QUOTE
"Teaching to the test is going to deny kids the education they deserve and need in the long run. It's like eating a candy bar before a race to get a boost of energy. A diet of candy bars won't work in the long run." *— Monty Neill, executive director of FairTest.*

Q. Whether we like it or not, students need to pass standardized tests to get into college. They can't wait for a more just and equitable world.

Students actually perform better on standardized tests when they have had a richer classroom experience. Assessments and practices that actually improve teaching and learning in kindergarten through high school will help students perform better on standardized measures.

Some people advocate a dual strategy: that we need to get rid of the reliance on standardized tests, while still ensuring that low-income students and students of color do well on these tests. Because of prejudice, discrimination and bias over time, many people of color and other disenfranchised people feel the need to demonstrate, without a doubt, that they are achieving at levels equal to their white and middle-class counterparts. And they are using standardized tests to demonstrate that achievement.

But ultimately, the problem is with the prejudice, discrimination, and bias in society at large. When students of color perform well on standardized tests, that doesn't guarantee equal access to quality education. Other forms of institutional prejudice and discrimination remain in place. ❏

A Harsh Agenda

High-stakes testing is being abused in the name of accountability – and almost always to the detriment of our children.

The following points are excerpted from a speech by Sen. Paul Wellstone (D-MN) at a conference in New York City in the Spring of 2000 on high-stakes testing. The complete text of Wellstone's remarks is available at www.rethinkingschools.org, under the section on standards and testing.

■ Education is, among other things, a process of shaping the moral imagination, character, skills and intellect of our children, of inviting them into the great conversation of our moral, cultural and intellectual life, and of giving them the resources to prepare to fully participate in the life of the nation and of the world. But today in education there is a threat afoot: the threat of high-stakes testing being grossly abused in the name of greater accountability — and almost always to the serious detriment of our children.

■ People talk about using tests to motivate students to do well and using tests to ensure that we close the achievement gap. This kind of talk is backwards and unfair. We cannot close the achievement gap until we close the gap in investment between poor and rich schools, no matter how "motivated" some students are. We know what these key investments are: quality teaching, parental involvement, and early childhood education, to name just a few.

■ It is simply negligent to force children to pass a test and expect that the poorest children, who face every disadvantage, will be able to do as well as those who have every advantage. When we do this, we hold children responsible for our own inaction and unwillingness to live up to our own promises and our own obligations. We confuse their failure with our own. This is a harsh agenda indeed for America's children.

■ Affording children an equal opportunity to learn is not enough. Even if all children had the opportunity to learn the material covered by the test, we still cannot close our eyes to the hard evidence that a single standardized test is not valid or reliable as the sole determinant in high-stakes decisions about students.

■ The effects of high-stakes testing go beyond their impact on individual students to greatly impact the educational process in general. They have had a deadening effect on learning. Studies indicate that public testing encourages teachers and administrators to focus instruction on test content, test format, and test preparation. Teachers tend to overemphasize the basic skills, and underemphasize problem-solving and complex thinking skills that are not well assessed on standardized tests. Further, they neglect content areas that are not covered such as science, social studies, and the arts. Stories are emerging from around the country about schools where teachers and students are under such pressure to perform that schools actually use limited funds to pay private companies to coach students and teachers in test-taking strategies.

■ Gunnar Myrdal said that ignorance is never random. If we do not know the impact of high-stakes tests, we can continue as we are now — sounding good while doing bad. High-stakes tests are part of an agenda that has been sweeping the nation. People use words like "accountability" and "responsibility" when they talk about high-stakes tests, but what they are being is anything but accountable or responsible. They do not see beyond their words to the harsh reality that underlies them and the harsh agenda that they are imposing on teachers, parents, and most of all, students.

■ The fight we confront today is not just a fight about tests, or just about ensuring that all our children are educated and educated well. It is time for us to renew our national vow of equal opportunity for every child in America. ❏

> *We cannot close the achievement gap until we close the gap in investment between poor and rich schools.*

Why Standardized Tests Are Bad

Decades of research have documented problems with standardized tests — from discrimination to diminished learning.

BY TERRY MEIER

No phenomenon poses a greater threat to educational equity, and ultimately to the quality of education in this country, than the escalating use of standardized achievement tests.

Fueled by public concern that schools are less rigorous than they used to be, standardized tests are increasingly prescribed as the "get tough" medicine needed to return excellence to our classrooms. Across the country, standardized tests are now routinely used to determine how and when students advance, from first grade through graduate school.

Standardized tests, which are notorious for their discriminatory effect on students of color, clearly threaten whatever small measures of educational equity have been won in recent decades. What is less obvious is that standardized tests threaten the educational experience of all children. The threat is so great, in fact, that standardized testing should be abolished.

Because standardized tests are a constant reality in students' lives, it is essential that parents understand the biases and limitations of such tests. Yet, as in so many other educational areas, parents are often excluded from the debate because they are deemed unable to understand the issue's complexity.

Tests are called "standardized" when the same test is given under similar conditions to large groups of students, whether district-wide, statewide, or nationwide. Most standardized tests ask multiple-choice questions and are corrected by a computer which recognizes only one "right" answer.

Decades of research have documented the biases in standardized tests, with students of color bearing the brunt of that discrimination. Across age groups, standardized tests discriminate against low-income students and students of color. While girls tend to do better on standardized tests at an early age, by high school and college their scores are on average below those of males, according to FairTest, a national group based in Cambridge, Mass., that lobbies against the growing use of standardized tests.

Advocates of testing argue that standardized achievement tests do not create inequities within schools, they merely reflect pre-existing inequities. According to this argument, children of color and low-income students tend to perform less well on standardized tests because they receive an inferior education.

Two false assumptions support this view. One is that standardized tests are a valid measure of excellence. The second is that standardized tests can be used to improve education, especially for low-income students and students of color.

> *Standardized tests tend to focus on lower-order skills*

No Real Connection to Excellence

Standardized achievement tests tend to focus on mechanical, lower-order skills and to reward students' rapid recognition of factual information. For example, standardized reading tests for young children stress phonics and the recognition of individual words. Research on learning to read, however, has shown the importance of integrating oral language, writing, reading, and spelling in a meaningful context that emphasizes children understanding what they read, not merely sounding out words. Similarly, research on teaching math stresses the importance of young children learning concepts through first-hand experience, while achievement tests for young children define math as knowing one's numbers.

Thus teachers face the dilemma of providing instruction that they know fosters a student's

Jean-Claude Lejeune

understanding, versus drilling students in isolated skills and facts that will help them do well on standardized tests.

It's not that students don't need to work on isolated skills sometimes, especially when they're first learning to read and write. But such work is only a means to the larger end of applying those skills in a meaningful context. Removed from context as they are on standardized tests, such skills are meaningless. Held up as a measure of achievement, they become mistaken for what is most important instead of what is ultimately trivial.

There is little, if any, connection between quality instruction and standardized test performance. Consider, for example, a successful high school English class in which students learn to write thoughtful, original essays in clear, concise language about topics they genuinely care about and that draw on their experiences. Assume that the teacher taught students to edit their work so that grammatical errors were rare.

Yet what does the American College Testing (ACT) Program test? Whether a student knows if the word "pioneered" is preferable to "started up by," or if "prove to be" is preferable to "come to be," or if "reach my destination" is preferable to "get there."

The point is that the choice is stylistic, dependent upon what one is trying to say and to whom. Removed from real life, the choice is meaningless. It reveals nothing about a student's com-

petence in reading and writing.

Consider another example, from a standardized reading achievement test where the child was asked to determine the "right" answer in the following selection:

> Father said: Once there was a land where boys and girls never grew up. They were always growing. What was Father telling?
> The truth___ A lie___ A story___

Any of these could be the "right" answer. If the father were speaking metaphorically, referring to mental and not physical growth, he could be telling the truth. It could also be a lie, for in black speech the word "lie" can also mean a joke or a story. And, of course, its initial "once" signals the conventions of fiction/fairy tales. (Hoover, Politzer, and Taylor, 1987, p. 91)

Standardized tests also ignore the skills and abilities needed to function in a complex, pluralistic society — such as the ability to work collectively in various social and cultural contexts, to adjust to change, to understand the perspectives of others, to persevere, to motivate, to solve problems in a real-life context, to lead, to value moral integrity and social commitment. As Harvard psychologist Howard Gardner points out, "there are hundreds and hundreds of ways to succeed, and many different abilities that will help you get there."

It is tragic that at the time when many developmental psychologists stress a broad and complex conception of intelligence and ability, and when one needs multiple talents to function effectively in the world, we have come to define excellence in our schools within the narrow parameters of what can be measured by standardized tests.

Clearly, standardized tests neither measure excellence nor foster it in our schools. So why the emphasis on such tests?

The fundamental reason is that the tests provide a seemingly objective basis upon which to allocate limited educational resources — to decide who gets into the best classes, high schools, or colleges. To that end, test items are deliberately selected so as to maximize differences between high and low scorers. By design, only some people will do well on the tests.

There can be little doubt that if a large percentage of white middle class students performed poorly on standardized tests, the test results would be viewed as invalid and discriminatory. There is no similar concern for students of color, despite some 25 years of extensive documentation of cultural bias in standardized testing.

Those who argue that it is possible to make standardized tests less discriminatory by removing their cultural bias seriously underestimate the enormity of their task. What is a "culture-fair" test in a multicultural society? And who could design such a test? The truth is that any knowledge worth having is inextricably linked to culture and to context — and thus can't be reduced to measurement on a standardized test.

In the final analysis, the most fundamental question to be answered about standardized testing is not why students of color tend to perform less well than white students, or even what can be done about it. Rather, the fundamental question is what is wrong with a society which allocates its educational resources on the basis of tests which not only fail to measure excellence, but which discriminate against the vast majority of its minority population? ❐

— Terry Meier is an associate professor in the Wheelock College Graduate School in Boston.

This article is condensed from an article that appeared originally in Rethinking Schools, Vol. 3, #2, Winter 1988. The full text of that article is available on-line at www.rethinkingschools.org, under "Past Issues."

NO COMMENT

A High-Stakes Environment

While teaching 10 years ago in the New York City public school system, I first learned what it is like to work in a high-stakes testing environment. It was not pretty.

The New York Board of Education's spring reading test was met with more anticipation than the Super Bowl. Individual school results and rankings were printed in all four New York City dailies. Parents and teachers made school choices based exclusively on these test results. And *The New York Times* has an annual feature lavishing praise on some inner-city school that had dramatically raised its scores.

I taught in one of those better achieving inner-city schools (a Harlem junior high), but my outlook wasn't as rosy as *The New York Times* feature writers'. In fact, I couldn't believe how early the "teaching for the test" began and how much it took over the curriculum.

Novels were kept on the shelves while students drilled on practice tests. Hallway bulletin boards promoted the coming test, and it wasn't unheard of for a school to have a reading test pep rally. Yes, many of the students raised their test scores because of the extensive preparation. But I doubt many of them became better readers. Instead of reading and discussing good books, students learned test-taking tips and memorized transitional phrases.

— Dan Forstner, an English teacher at Humboldt Junior High in St. Paul, writing in the June 6, 2000, St. Paul Pioneer Press.

Origins of the Latest Testing Craze

During the Civil Rights era, equal opportunity was a driving force in education reform. Today it's accountability and standards.

BY BARBARA MINER

The current push for standards and standard-ized tests has its political origins in the 1983 *A Nation at Risk* report. Released during the economic recession of the early 1980s (and during the Reagan Administration's attack on the social movements of the 1960s and 1970s), the report sounded an alarmist cry that our country's economic viability was in jeopardy due to a "rising tide of mediocrity" in our schools.

Before long, accountability and high standards overtook what at least rhetorically had been a top policy consideration in public education since the Civil Rights Movement: equal opportunity.

Presidents George Bush and Bill Clinton continued the push for standards and test-driven reform with their Goals 2000 and calls for national standards and tests. They were stymied, however, by opposition from the far right and the left. The right was loath to agree to any federal role in education, and progressives feared that without an emphasis on resources and increased opportunities to learn, national tests would victimize low–income students and students of color.

> *Currently, 49 states have state standards, up from 14 in 1996.*

In 1996, test-driven reform found new life. Corporate leaders began to assert strong leadership and the movement, while still national in scope, implemented a state-based strategy. That year, Louis Gerstner Jr., head of IBM, co-hosted a National Education Summit with Wisconsin Governor Tommy Thompson (R). The summit set a more focused agenda based on standards and testing to be implemented by the states, and the movement for test-driven reform took off (see article p. 114).

Many professional organizations and local schools and districts had been involved earlier in the 1990s in standards-based reform. By the decade's end, however, the standards movement was dominated by corporate and political forces. While "opportunity to learn" had been an important part of initial discussions on standards — the view that without equal opportunity, equal outcomes were an illusion — that perspective soon took a back seat to the emphasis on "results."

Currently, 49 states have established state standards in core academic subjects, up from 14 in 1996. (Iowa is the only hold-out, prompting author and anti-testing advocate Alfie Kohn to comment, "Thank God for Iowa.") Further, a growing number of states — 27 at last count — are implementing high-stakes tests.

In analyzing the latest testing craze, one must look at the cultural, economic, and political climate. As many articles in this booklet note, standardized tests have historically been used to legitimize social inequality. In this era of growing inequality, test scores provide a way to rationalize why some students and schools get more resources and some get fewer. In addition, the standards movement, as it has evolved, also provides a way to counteract the multiculturalism movement and to re-assert a more traditional, Eurocentric view of what students should learn.

As standardized tests are increasingly equated with reform, however, a backlash is growing among parents, teachers, and students who argue that educational achievement is far more complicated than what can be measured in a single test. While slogans such as "no social promotion" and "high-standards for all" make for good media soundbites, they are falling short as programs of reform.

As C. Thomas Holmes, a University of Georgia education professor who is a leading researcher on the topic, notes: "Parents are all for retention, until it's their kid." ❑

At Best, Silly, At Worst, Racist

The Massachusetts 10th-grade world history test is a Eurocentric exercise in trivial pursuit.

BY
DERRICK Z. JACKSON

The difference between a diploma and doomsday cannot possibly come down to a Byzantine trivial pursuit. That is, unless you can make the implausible case that six or seven years from now, when these students are trembling job applicants, their bosses will look them dead in the eye and actually ask:

"Hmmm, your resume looks interesting, but to get this job you must tell me why King Henry issued the Edict of Nantes, the purpose of the Treaty of Tordesillas, and the function of the lord of the estate in medieval Europe."

Those are real — or surreal — requests of students from last month's Massachusetts Comprehensive Assessment System 10th-grade history and social sciences test. Some educators let me read the full test last week.

Many parents, educators, and business leaders are already concerned about the more subjective aspects of the MCAS. Some have called for any high-stakes testing for graduation in 2003 to be limited to basic literacy and math.

The 10th-grade history test should call into question the political intentions of the entire test. At best, it is silly. At worst, it is racist.

The test, which focuses on "world" history, has 57 items. There are 12 slightly different forms of the test. Of the 57 items, about 40 refer to Europe, from the Byzantine Empire to the Cold War. Five are questions about capitalism. Only 12 are about the rest of the world.

For Europe, students needed specifics on wars, innovations, cities, and individual writers, economists, and artists. They had to know, "In 1429, which military commander led a French army that defeated the English at Orleans? A. Joan of Arc; B. Catherine the Great; C. Napoleon Bonaparte; D. Charlemagne."

In fact, the MCAS really should be renamed the Mutual Charlemagne Admiration Society. The founder of the first empire in western Europe after the fall of Rome was also in this question: "Many separate groups attacked Charlemagne's empire. The fiercest of these groups came from the north and was known as the A. Magyars; B. Visig

> ## NO COMMENT
>
> The fourth grade test of the Massachusetts Comprehensive Assessment System is about 14 hours — one hour more than the Massachusetts bar exam.

Wasseram/L.A. Times Syndicate

oths; C. Huns; D. Vikings."

Students were given detailed maps of Eurasia and asked if the dotted routes represent the Crusades or the spice trade. About all students got for Africa was a bare outline of the continent and asked to point out the desert — where there are no people to have a history. Asians are reduced to shoguns, samurais, and the split between China and Taiwan. Latin America is but a colonial appendage of Europe, and women, other than Joan of Arc and Catherine the Great, are almost invisible.

One teacher told me the heads of black and brown students of color slumped lower and lower during the history test. "We work so hard at teaching them useful information and critical thinking skills and then we give them a test that tells them that their people are nothing," she said. "It's crushing."

Telling African-American and Latino students their history is worth nothing is having a crushing effect. The failure rate for African-American and Latino students on last year's 8th-grade history test was 77 percent and 85 percent, respectively, higher than even their well-publicized failure rates in math. The effect is so crushing that questions must be answered before the state can proceed to the 2003 deadline for any section of the test. It is not enough to can the history part, for it may also be a Freudian slip about math and English. Is it a mere coincidence that the same state that so easily renders people of color nonexistent in world history also has no plan to give failing students the courses they need to pass the 10th grade math test?

A test that shows if students are literate is fine. A test that is mired in a trivially narrow vision of yesterday is cruel. American thinker William James said, "Things learned thus in a few hours, on one occasion, for one purpose, cannot possibly have formed many associations with other things in the mind. Their brain-processes are led into by few paths, and are relatively little liable to be awakened again. Speedy oblivion is the almost inevitable fate of all that is committed to memory in this simple way."

Speedy oblivion is where the MCAS history test should go. On Friday, you can decide for yourself with questions from the 10th grade MCAS history and social sciences test (see article page 24). ❏

—Derrick Z. Jackson is a columnist for The Boston Globe.

The above article appeared in the June 7, 2000, Boston Globe and is reprinted with permission.

Welcome to Measurement Inc.

In a renovated factory in the heart of tobacco country, low-wage, part-time workers grade essays and pass judgment on millions of youths.

BY
DAVID GLOVIN

DURHAM, NC — In the heart of tobacco country, in a boxy brick building sandwiched between tire stores and a sprawling factory, you can find Ground Zero of New Jersey's education reform movement.

And Texas'. And Maryland's. And, in total, two dozen states'.

This is where essays from standardized tests come to be scored. On a single day in November, 70 paid graders working for the private firm Measurement Inc. scored 11,908 essays from New Jersey high school students. Sitting for seven hours a day in rooms that resemble large classrooms, they collectively pass judgment each year on the writing skills of millions of American students. They do not get rich at wages of $7.25 to $7.75 an hour, without benefits, but for many the flexibility is enough to offset the monotony.

But don't expect to find teachers here. Ron Tanner is an ex-fighter pilot who has scored 150,000 essays in three years. Jeff Haubner is a recent college graduate who came to Durham in search of work. Karen Anderson scored papers as she was launching her art gallery.

All told, they're a collection of college-educated jobbers who earn extra cash by evaluating the writing of the country's youth. And because it's here, and in six other scoring sites, where the essay portion of 4 million high-stakes standardized exams is graded, they are the ones who help determine who graduates, gets promoted, or is held back for remediation.

Surprised? Educators in New Jersey were. Not one of a dozen teachers or administrators interviewed, including several who managed testing programs, knew who scored the essays on these exams. All assumed that the graders were teachers or other professional educators.

Measurement Inc. says errors in grading are the exception and that virtually all papers are scored accurately by the part-time scorers. "I wondered ... how professional people would be," said Tanner, the former pilot. "But it's incredible how seriously people take it. We're not just scoring papers. We're scoring people."

Growing Use of Essays

All but two states — Nebraska and Iowa — now use standardized tests to measure student achievement. For years, states required only that students shade in answer grids to multiple choice questions. Quick to grade and with one correct answer, they offered a fast snapshot of student achievement and were not subject to whims of individual graders.

But critics said these tests measure only memorization and test-taking skill. Essays, on the other hand, force students to reason and compose logical thoughts.

"Educators generally consider that [essays] tap more complex skills, more higher-ended skills," said Gregory Camilli, an education professor at Rutgers University in New Jersey. "Educators also want these tests to send a message about what's valued by the state "— in this case, writing.

"After 20 years of schooling, your aptitude test shows that you're skilled at just one thing — taking tests."

Today, 42 states include essays on the standardized exams that they give to students in elementary, middle, or high school, according to the publication *Education Week*. That's millions of essays each year. Somebody needs to grade them.

For some states, local teachers grade them. For others, Karen Anderson did.

Looking for extra money as she was launching her art studio, Anderson worked at Measurement Inc. in 1995, and she recalls the endless hours she spent pouring over student essays in Measurement's Durham headquarters. "It was the most boring job I ever had," she said.

"These papers are not that interesting," she added. "To sit in a chair each day and read the same simplistic thoughts — it made you lose faith in the way people wrote."

Yet Anderson took her job seriously, reading every paper from start to finish. "I never skipped over anything," she said. And she had only praise for her colleagues, some of whom were professionals with master's degrees.

But there were others at Measurement Inc. who were less conscientious. Just ask Julian Harrison.

Harrison, a free-lance photographer who graded papers for three years until 1993, said he read 10,700 papers in one two-month period. "There were times I'd be reading a paper every 10 seconds," he said. "It was horrific."

At one point, Harrison would only briefly scan papers before issuing a grade, searching for clues such as a descriptive passage within a narrative to determine what grade to give. "You could skim them very quickly. You could read them very fast," said Harrison. "You could actually — I know this sounds very bizarre — but you could put a number on these things without actually reading the paper."

The same quality-control measures that the company used when Anderson read papers were there when Harrison graded essays, and they're still used today. Still, like other readers, Harrison felt pressured to read his share of papers — and to get the $200 bonus that kicked in after 8,000 papers.

He knows he gave some papers the wrong grade.

"Either I read it too fast or I didn't recognize what the child [meant] or maybe I got impatient because the child's handwriting was very bad," he said. "Maybe some of the readers weren't careful enough, and maybe a child got a three instead of a four or a two instead of a four. Or maybe they failed."

Measurement is among a handful of firms that develop and grade standardized tests and their essays, earning upwards of $6 for each paper it scores. In the month before testing season — usually late Spring, occasionally in the Fall — the firm advertises in local newspapers and on radio for part-timers looking to earn extra cash.

Measurement will interview almost anyone with a college degree, but it then employs a sophisticated monitoring process that constantly scans graders' work to ensure that scoring is consistent among graders. The graders score up to 45,000 papers each day during peak season in the Spring. Sitting two to a table, they grade an average of 150 papers in a seven-hour day, although some go over 200.

Jean-Claude Lejeune

Is this the best way to score such important exams? Company officials say it is, and testing experts say the firm uses sound methods. Every paper is read at least twice.

Why Not Teachers?

But teachers ask if it makes sense to use part-timers working in a former headache powder factory, far away from students' schools. "You would think people in education would be selected," said Joan Pra Sisto, a guidance counselor in the city of Passaic, NJ. "We know what we're looking for."

Neha Rana also has her doubts. The teenager took the writing test last October and was crushed when the results came back. "After they told me I failed, I started crying," Neha said. "The school switched my classes. They put me down from A-level classes to C-level classes."

There was one problem, though: Neha should have passed. In the rush to score the essays, graders mistakenly failed her and three classmates. She was pulled from a class where she wrote research papers and spent months in remedial classes. After Neha's school district asked Measurement to re-check her score, the firm caught its error.

High Stakes

Under the gun to produce high scores, it's not just Neha who knows the importance of these tests. Superintendents may lose their jobs and trustees may lose elections, if schools don't measure up.

So schools have responded. A principal in Ridgewood, NJ, a tiny town with one of the top schools in the state, said his middle school now focuses less on in-depth writing and more on the quick essays demanded on the tests. Passaic is not the only district to banish failing students to remedial classes, and teachers in Paterson, NJ, a struggling urban district, say they're less likely to teach poetry and creative writing so they can concentrate on the exam.

In fact, in what some fear will actually lead to a dumbing down of writing, many New Jersey schools now emphasize a five-paragraph essay format that they believe satisfies test graders — an introduction, three supporting paragraphs, and a conclusion. Paterson educators say that's how they got a surge in writing scores, and other schools are using the same method.

"We're basically making sure that our students write an essay in the format test graders want," said James Bender, the superintendent in Little Falls, NJ. ❐

— David Glovin is a senior education writer for The Record of Hackensack, NJ, where an extended version of this story originally ran.

This story is printed with the permission of The Record. The article also appeared in Rethinking Schools, Vol. 13, #3, Spring 1999.

FAILING OUR KIDS:
WHY THE TESTING CRAZE WON'T FIX OUR SCHOOLS

AP Photo/Angela Rowlings

Parents and Students Talk Back

MCAS Test Draws Fire

A parent activist explains why parents have petitioned, rallied, and called boycotts to protest Massachusetts' high-stakes tests.

BY
JACKIE DEE KING

Hundreds of students, including about 150 in Cambridge, boycotted the MCAS in April and May. Hundreds of parents and students rallied on the Boston Common May 15, 2000 to protest the exam. They delivered petitions bearing almost 7,000 signatures to the Governor's office, information packets to every legislator, and vowed to return next year with enough petitions to wrap around the State House.

Why are so many people so upset?

The MCAS is given to students in 4th, 8th, and 10th grades in English language arts, math, science and social studies. Next year's 10th graders will have to pass the English and math portions of the test by the year 2003 in order to graduate from high school.

The nine-member, non-elected state Board of Education claims that the MCAS is the only way to hold students and school systems accountable. Since passage of the 1993 Education Reform Act, about $2 billion in additional funding has been made available to schools. The Board of Ed says the only way to ensure the money is being spent responsibly is to give students one big standardized test.

If they fail — as more than 53% of them did statewide in 1998 — many students will be placed in low-tracked remediation courses, summer schools, and weekend test preparation centers. Many will have to keep taking the test over and over if they want a shot at graduating from high school.

Who's being held accountable?

The accountability argument does not impress Larry Ward, who is father of three daughters in the Cambridge public schools. "You tell me how it's holding the school system accountable, if they end up pushing a whole section of the population out of school, especially low-income and minority children," he said. "If you want to talk about accountability, let's start at the top, with state and local officials responsible for education, not with those who are most vulnerable on the bottom."

"We do not have a level playing field in this society," Ward noted. "Urban school systems such as Boston's continue to have many overcrowded classes with more than 30 kids, courses with no textbooks or other vital materials, labs with no running water, deteriorating buildings, and overstressed and sometimes undertrained teachers. Let's put the resources directly into the schools instead of into a test that punishes the kids."

Many of the students who boycotted the MCAS were led to that action by the test's discriminatory impact upon students of color, according to Hannah Jukovsky, one of the 10th grade leaders of the boycott at Cambridge Ridge and Latin High School, "We were outraged when we saw that 80% of African-Americans and 83% of Latinos statewide failed the 10th grade math test," she said. "We students get it: some kids are just considered disposable."

Parents and students in both suburban and urban areas have also been disturbed by the deadening impact the MCAS has on curriculum. In-depth, exploratory courses are being replaced with broad survey courses, a mile wide and an inch deep, which require students to memorize large amounts of material they will soon forget. Electives are being eliminated at some schools. "A meaningful, rich curriculum is just as important for inner-city kids who may be struggling academically as it is for suburban kids," Ward said. "A diet of drill-and-kill exercises will eventually drive kids out of school. We need courses that engage the students, keep them in school, and turn them into life-long learners who can succeed in the world."

The state has announced plans to spread the test to more grades and to require passing scores in more subjects in exchange for a diploma. The MCAS takes about 18 hours in the upper grades; it is far longer than the Massachusetts' Bar Exam, the Medical Boards, or the Graduate Record Exams. The MCAS is not a basic skills test; it is pitched at a much more difficult level. Many educators believe the test is deeply flawed: full of ambiguously worded and tricky questions, culturally biased, and arbitrarily graded.

The MCAS represents an especially unfair barrier for special education students, vocational ed students, and students with limited English proficiency, all of whom have to take the same test as other students. "Many vocational students are having to put aside their valuable, complex courses in rebuilding engines or designing computer programs so they can drill for the kinds of questions asked on the MCAS," Jukovsky said. Ward concluded, "If I had to ask one question, I'd say this: How can you deny a student a diploma based on

AP Photo/Angela Rowlings

Hundreds of students from across Massachusetts boycotted the state's high-stakes test in April 2000. Above, students at Brookline High School protest outside their school.

the results of one paper-and-pencil test, especially one with as many problems as this?"

Boycotts are tip of iceberg

The boycotts were only the most dramatic form of the growing opposition to the test. Since last spring, anti-MCAS parents groups have sprung up in many Greater Boston communities, including Cambridge, Boston, Arlington, Brookline, Newton, Wayland, Somerville, New Bedford, and in cities and towns throughout Western Massachusetts, where forums have consistently drawn 150-200 people. Most of the groups are part of the statewide Coalition for Authentic Reform in Education, or CARE. ❐

— Jackie King, an Area 4 resident, is the mother of two sons at the Graham and Parks School. She and Larry Ward have been active in the Cambridge MassParents group and have recently taken positions as organizers for the Coalition for Authentic Reform in Education.

To contact MassParents, the Cambridge chapter of CARE, call 617-441-0863 or visit the website at www.massparents. org or subscribe to the listserv by sending a blank email message to: massparents-subscribe@igc.topica.com

'No' Is the Right Answer

A high school student explains why she refused to take the Massachusetts Comprehensive Assessment Test.

BY ELEANOR MARTIN

On May 17, [1999] a dozen sophomores at Cambridge Ridge and Latin High School decided not to take the state-mandated Massachusetts Comprehensive Assessment Test, better known as the MCAS. I was one of them.

For weeks we had carefully researched the political and moral issues at stake. We were aware that it was going to be difficult to refuse the test. When you are a sophomore in high school, it is not easy to go against the orders of your teachers, your advisors, your school, and your state. We were not certain of the punishment that we would receive. Detention, suspension, expulsion? All had been mentioned as possibilities.

When we announced what we were going to do, we received a lot of opposition. We were told that we were going to bring down the cumulative score of our house and of the entire school. But we believed, and still do, that the reasons for fighting this test are more important than any score.

Beginning with the class of 2003, high school students who fail the MCAS test will not be able to graduate. We believe that a single test should not determine the success and future of a student.

How can four years of learning and growing be assessed by a single standardized test? There are so many things that students learn throughout high school — how to play an instrument, act, draw, paint. They learn photography, how to program a computer, fix a car engine, cook tortellini Alfredo, throw a pot, or design a set for a play. Many students say these are among the most important skills they learn in high school, yet all are skills the MCAS fails to recognize.

The MCAS test is expected to take over 20 hours of class time. No test should take that much time out of learning, especially not one whose supposed rationale is that students are not learning enough in school.

The material on the MCAS is very specific. For students to do well, teachers must redesign their curriculums to teach to the test. Districts and school administrators, eager to show high scores, have pressured teachers to create units based on the material. Because the test is based largely on memorization of facts, teachers will have to teach their students these specific facts instead of teaching for deep comprehension and understanding of the material.

Students who have been in this country for only three years are required to take the test. How can someone who has been speaking English for three years be expected to write essays with correct spelling and grammar, which is a requirement to receive a proficient score? Special needs students are also required to take this test to graduate.

Supposedly, this test will be used to evaluate teachers as well as students. However, a test like this simply measures whether a teacher teaches to the test.

If the MCAS test is instituted in Massachusetts, the scores will become a major consideration for parents when they choose a school for their children. Schools will therefore want their scores to be as high as possible. Programs such as Metco, which integrates inner-city students into suburban schools, may be discouraged since it has been shown that inner-city students do not score as well as suburban students.

We are also concerned about the future of innovative programs, such as the Interactive Math Program, or IMP, which does not follow the traditional progression of algebra, geometry, trigonom-

> **How can four years of learning and growing be assessed by a single standardized test?**

etry, and calculus, but integrates these throughout all four years. Therefore, a sophomore IMP student will not know the expected geometry curriculum, but will know some trigonometry and calculus that is not included on the MCAS.

Also, certain in-depth courses, such as "Bible as Literature," "The Holocaust," "Reading and Writing on Human Values," "Women in Literature," and "African-American Literature" will no doubt be off-limits to freshmen and sophomores because they are not geared to the MCAS.

My humanities teacher in eighth grade used the "Facing History and Ourselves" curriculum, which spends about eight weeks teaching in incredible depth about the Holocaust. We learned about Nazi propaganda and how it compares to propaganda used today. We examined the causes of the Holocaust, confronted the difficult philosophical and moral issues it raises, and focused on what we can do to prevent it from happening again.

This is one of the best educational experiences I have ever had. Because of it, I have a deep and complex understanding of the Holocaust. All the dates and facts that I learned may not stay with me, but I feel certain that my understanding of the event will.

We are worried that such innovative and respected curriculums as IMP and "Facing History" will become casualties of the MCAS test mentality.

We are not saying nothing should be done to improve public education in Massachusetts. We are simply saying that taking a paper and pencil test to graduate is not the way to amend education. Massachusetts has already spent $24 million on the MCAS test, and an estimated $14 million more is being spent this year. Roughly that same amount will be spent every year the test is given. We could use that money in better ways — for more staff developers, teacher workshops, improved bilingual education, better school supplies, and better fine arts and technical arts programs.

This is our last chance to raise awareness about getting an education that is not standardized, but meaningful, deep, and personalized. We believe an education like that is worth working for. ❒

— Eleanor Martin is an honors student at Cambridge Ridge and Latin High School.

The above is reprinted with permission from the Boston Globe, where it appeared as a commentary.

Chicago's Flunking Policy Gets an 'F'

"No Social Promotion" is the rallying cry of Chicago reform. What's really happening?

BY JULIE WOESTEHOFF

CHICAGO — Across the country, politicians are citing Chicago as an example of how policies of "no social promotion" are the answer to the troubles of urban school systems. Let a Chicago parent activist take you in for a closer look at this "get tough" policy that flunks thousands of students every year.

I am the parent of one recent Chicago Public School (CPS) graduate and a CPS high school student. I am also a former member of two local school councils and have been involved for 10 years with Parents United for Responsible Education (PURE), where I am currently executive director. PURE was founded in 1987 to strengthen the parents' role in decision-making in the Chicago schools.

Chicago was the first major urban district to institute an extensive "no social promotion" policy. Since 1997, Chicago has required third– sixth– and eighth-grade students who did not meet necessary scores on the standardized test known as the Iowa Tests of Basic Skills (ITBS) to attend a "summer bridge" program and be retested at summer's end. Most of those who again failed the tests were retained in their grade or, if they were 15, sent to "transition centers." Under a special waiver policy, certain students were promoted even if they failed the test.

Data over the years shows that about 50,000 students have been asked to repeat a grade, based on their ITBS scores. Yet the margin of error in the ITBS is so precarious that even one wrong answer can make as much as nine months' difference in an eighth-grade student's grade equivalent score. (The district refuses to allow students to graduate if they are even one month below the cut-off score.)

Educational researchers have documented the dangers of flunking kids — that retention contributes to greater academic failure in the long run, to higher levels of dropping out, and to increased discipline problems. In Chicago, the problem of increased drop-out rates surfaced quickly. According to a November 1998 study by the non-profit advocacy group Designs for Change, high school freshman enrollment dropped that year even though district enrollment was increasing. More than 1,000 potential freshmen could not be accounted for. In recent years, the number of "missing" high school students has increased. High school enrollment has dropped by about 10,000 since 1995, at the same time as overall school enrollment has increased by 30,000; such numbers cannot be explained merely by changes in demographics.

PURE has also asked the district to investigate allegations of rampant cheating on the ITBS tests. PURE argues that the cheating is essentially encouraged by the district, which insists that schools "clean" all student test score sheets before turning them in, which is considered tampering in other districts.

Recent Developements

Two recent developments have added to the controversy over Chicago's policy of retaining thousands.

First, the Office for Civil Rights of the U.S. Department of Education agreed in November 1999 to investigate complaints that the use of the ITBS to determine retention is disproportionately discriminatory against African-American and Latino students. Second, a report in December 1999 by the Consortium on Chicago School Research gave the "no social promotion policy" mixed reviews. A leading member of the consortium issued a minority statement calling the Chicago program "a failure."

The federal civil rights complaint was filed by PURE and individual parents of Chicago students. The suit alleges that the district's use of ITBS test scores as sole measures to determine student promotion and retention violates federal legal and civil rights laws and principles. PURE also alleges that application of the district's waiver policy, under which some students are promoted even if they do not pass the ITBS, is arbitrary and discriminatory.

PURE found that the enrollment of African-American and Latino students in transition centers is disproportionately high compared with their enrollment in the general school population. Donald Moore, executive director of Designs for Change, has released figures showing that African-American students are four-and-a-half times more likely to be retained than white students, and Latino students are nearly three times more likely to be retained than white students.

PURE is asking that the district revise its promotion policy so that students will be evaluated on multiple measures of learning. It also asks for a clearly written, non-discriminatory waiver policy that includes due process. PURE and other groups have won some concessions from district officials, who now say they are changing the promotion policy to include other measures besides ITBS scores. However, no proposal for a revised policy has been made public.

Report Gives Mixed Reviews

In December 1999, the Consortium on Chicago School Research released its first report on the effects of the no social promotion policy on student achievement and school instruction. The Consortium is an independent federation of Chicago area organizations that conducts research on Chicago's public schools.

The report indicated that retained students continue to achieve extremely poorly on the Iowa Test, even after a summer school intensively focused on test-taking and after repeating a grade during the regular school year. "While summer bridge raised students' performance briefly, there is no evidence that it altered the overall pattern of school-year achievement for these students," the report said.

The report also found increases in the proportion of students who meet the test-score cutoff for promotions — which district officials are hailing as a sign of success while ignoring how an unrelenting emphasis on standardized tests distorts teaching and learning and encourages cheating. Finally, the report gave mixed results on whether getting students to meet the minimum score allows them to do better the next year; and it noted the uneven access across schools to policy waivers.

In a minority report, Consortium Steering Committee member Donald Moore argued that both the retention policy and the social promotion policy it replaced are failures. He called for alternatives for improving student achievement and cited in particular the need for quality early childhood education, improved reading instruction in early grades, and replicating the practices of high-achieving inner-city schools in other schools. ⊐

— Julie Woestehoff is the executive director of Parents United for Responsible Education, a nonprofit advocacy group involved in Chicago school reform.

Wasserman/L.A. Times Syndicate

Students Say 'Enough!'

Chicago high schoolers say they will no longer 'feed the test-taking frenzy.'

The following is the text of the letter from students at Whitney Young High School explaining why they deliberately failed the Illinois Goals Assessment Program test. This letter was distributed at Whitney Young in February 1999 at the time of the tests.

To Whom It May Concern:

Some concerned students are weary of standardized tests and all of the baggage with which they come. Although tests are useful for giving some sort of "objective" account of some types of achievement, enough is enough. This year, the junior class has wasted a significant amount of class time preparing for and taking three different standardized tests. Since we have been in high school, we have taken probably ten, including the PSAT, IGAP, TAP, CASE, NEDT, and several others whose names have been forgotten in the swirl of acronyms. The actual administration of the test is not the only problem; the whole school day on which the test comes is wasted because the shortened periods do not allow teachers enough time to accomplish anything and many teachers do not want to give work that might conceivably cause stress during the tests. An inordinate amount of time is also consumed in the preparation teachers are forced to give us before each test. All this time could be spent giving us a real education instead of teaching us how to take multiple-choice tests.

Of even greater concern is the message Whitney Young's emphasis on test scores gives to students. Pressuring everybody to do well on the tests makes people think that the tests are much more important than they really are. Most of these tests measure very narrow types of learning; there is a definite skill to answering multiple-choice questions that is independent of any useful education, and even the essays are very specifically formatted to see how well we can regurgitate the five-paragraph format drilled into our heads since grammar school. You, the administration and the school board, are telling us that these are the skills we should be pursuing. Free thought and originality seem to have no place in the tests that you so proudly parade as proof of Whitney Young's and the Chicago Public School system's excellence.

The consequences of this foolhardy stress on test scores reach into the self-confidence of many. Students know the administration of the school is preoccupied with test scores. Many of our academic teachers have some sort of test score right next to our names on the roster. That score is the first impression they have of us; we are reduced to numbers. Countless students consider themselves "dumb" merely because a multiple-choice test tells them they are. High-achieving students compare test scores with each other and feel they have to compete to see who can get the best mark. Sometimes it seems people live up to the expectations placed on them. If you continue to tell students who do not score well on tests that their scores show they are deficient, they will continue to do poorly on the tests and often in their classes as well. It is a vicious spiral perpetuated by the administration of this school and the school system.

To the administration of Whitney Young, we do understand that these tests are forced upon the school. However, the proper response to harmful requirements is to largely ignore them. We do not need to be spending time preparing for these tests and in doing so further legitimizing them in the minds of both students at Whitney Young and administrators at the Board of Education. In a Student Union meeting at which this issue was brought up, you told us you had done all you could, and it was time for us to take action. Now we are.

That is why some students will fail the IGAP today. We refuse to feed this test-taking frenzy. We ask that the time and energy spent on standardized tests be reduced to the minimum possible. Teachers should be discouraged from teaching the answers to the tests except when the skills and knowledge form a part of the curriculum those teachers are trying to teach. The school and the school system should show its academic superiority through the quality of its education and the accomplishments of its students rather than the numbers on its test scores. ❏

— *Will Tanzman et al.*

The above is reprinted from Rethinking Schools, Vol. 13, #4, Summer 1999.

Jean-Claude Lejeune

NO COMMENT

Forced Test-taking

In an effort to stymie a student boycott of the high-stakes test in Massachusetts last May, school officials at the High School of Science and Technolgoy in Springfield packed hundreds of 10th graders into the cafeteria under false pretenses. They then admistered the exam to students, who were sitting elbow to elbow in groups of eight at round tables. Many students talked openly and shared answers.

"One teacher wept over the situation," according to a report in the Massachusetts News. "A vice principal shouted at students to 'shut up.'"

"I tell you, if the state came in and saw that, they would have null and voided that test completely," one teacher said.

Testing Slights Multiculturism

Matthew Henson is out; Christopher Columbus is in.

BY MAKANI THEMBA-NIXON

As a parent active on a local school council, I've watched with apprehension as Virginia's high-stakes testing program has unfolded. But it was not until the day my third grade son came home sad and dejected that I realized my worst fears about the test were true.

My son's class was studying explorers — his favorite subject — and he wanted to write a report on Matthew Henson, his favorite explorer. Henson, an African–American, was the first man to set foot on the North Pole. He was a self-taught sailor and astronomer who rose above the racism and prejudice of his day to become one of the most important explorers of the 20th century.

Imagine my thrill as my son, without any urging on my part, went to the computer to do research on Henson. I was particularly pleased because after a tough first grade and difficulty reading in second grade, in third grade my son was at last learning that school could be fun.

While researching on the computer, my son took great delight in finding obscure facts about Henson. He fantasized out loud about how impressed his teachers and classmates would be once they saw his great report.

I had never seen him so excited about school work. He really identified with Henson, not only because he and Henson are both African–Americans, which was clearly important to him, but also because he was excited about the opportunity to be an explorer himself. What excited him most was the novelty of the information and the fact that Henson wasn't one of the explorers the class as a whole was studying. As he said to me, "Mom, I'm being an explorer in social studies!"

When he turned in his report, he got a much different reaction than he expected. His teacher patiently explained that although his hard work was obvious and it was a great report, he would have to do another report on Christopher Columbus instead.

It turns out that Matthew Henson isn't on Virginia's high-stakes test, known as the Standards of Learning (SOL).

Like any mother, I called the teacher. I tried hard to be understanding. She said she felt bad about her decision and admitted that she knew what it meant to my son to be so excited about school. But, she rationalized, it wasn't her fault. She was trying to make sure he passed the Virginia test. After all, so much was on the line.

In that regard, she is right. The SOLs are high-stakes with winners and many more losers.

The tests, and the curriculum acrobatics schools undertake to adapt to them, literally determine what's important to know and what's not. Books, methods, and coursework that don't support test standards are thrown by the wayside. For example, students at my children's elementary school who do not meet SOLs in math must forego art classes for extra tutoring. And, of course, any historical figures that don't fit within the mostly white framework of the state standards are lost as well.

I worry about my children in this new world of high-stakes testing. How will they remain creative or sustain an interest in lifelong learning? Further, if the tests are to ensure that our students are better prepared, it's completely confounding that multicultural education is ignored in the development of learning standards. ❐

> *Why is a multicultural approach ignored in the development of standards?*

— *Makani Themba-Nixon is director of the Grass Roots Innovative Policy Program of the Applied Research Center and author of Making Policy, Making Change: How Communities Are Taking Law Into Their Own Hands.*

The above is reprinted from Rethinking Schools, Vol. 14, #3, Spring 2000.

We Object

Parents of fourth-grade students explain why they believe Massachusetts' standardized tests do more harm than good.

BY STEVE COHEN, LINDA NATHAN, PAT HERRINGTON, DAWN SHEARER COREN, MARGERY WILSON, AND TIM WISE

We, the parents of six fourth-graders at Cambridgeport elementary school, are refusing to allow our children to take the MCAS [Massachusetts Comprehensive Assessment System] tests. Instead, on May 17 [1999] we began an alternative, parent-led curriculum for our children during the testing periods to protest the excessive class time devoted to a standardized test that we feel does much more harm than good for public education in Massachusetts.

We have taken this dramatic step because we strongly object to the way in which the MCAS test has come to dominate the fourth-grade curriculum in the spring. Despite teachers' conscientious efforts to limit its impact, the MCAS testing will take at least 20 hours of class time, not counting preparation and recovery time. We feel this is time that should be spent learning math, reading, spelling, and other important subjects, rather than learning how to score well on standardized tests on those subjects. We object to the clearly negative impact this is having on our children's education.

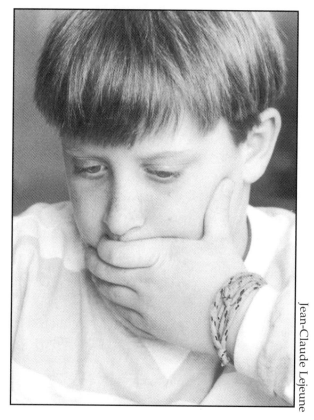

Jean-Claude Lejeune

A Richer Experience

By refusing to allow our children to be tested, we are providing them with a far richer educational experience than marathon test-taking, and we are protesting the imposition of this particularly excessive and inappropriate assessment tool. We all strongly believe in high standards and performance-based assessment, but feel the MCAS undermines both.

Dr. Deborah Meier, founder of the Mission Hill Elementary School and the first public school teacher to win a MacArthur Foundation "genius" award, put it well in a statement issued last year by a committee of educators: "Success for all kids — rich and poor — requires high standards linked to rigorous, performance-based assessment. The path the MCAS leads us on will not reach this vital goal. Instead it will weaken the quality of many schools and do little to cause real improvements where they are needed."

The Cambridgeport School administration has discouraged our action, but neither we nor our children are being threatened with punitive measures, as have others in the state who have refused to take the test. According to the state's policies, however, our school will be "punished" by having non-participating students (who represent about 15% of fourth-graders in the school) scored "zero" instead of "absent." This will, therefore, depress the results reported for the school in what is emerging as the annual competition among Massachusetts schools to see which can score best on the MCAS tests. We reject that competition and urge any who doubt the quality of education being practiced at Cambridgeport School to come look at the impressive portfolios each child has, a collection of work that represents a truly comprehensive assessment of learning. ❏

The above is reprinted from Rethinking Schools, Vol. 14, #1, Fall 1999.

My Daughter, Child #008458743

BY JEFF ZORN

After a two-month delay, California parents, educators, and newspapers finally got the results of last spring's STAR (Standardized Testing and Reporting). Probably no group was more deeply affected than the parents of the youngest students tested, the second graders.

My own daughter, Sarah Jane, heretofore a winsome if silly denizen of my household, was suddenly redefined as "Child #008458743." Her school, a Chinese Language Immersion School, became School #6113245.

Sarah Jane's permanent record now shows where she stands, on a percentile basis, among American children on particular subskills of language and mathematics. A more educationally worthless and civically damaging conception of children like Sarah Jane cannot be imagined.

STAR features Harcourt-Brace's Stanford 9 test, administered this year to over 4.5 million California public school students in grades two through 11. Sarah Jane's Stanford 9 scores told nothing useful about her intellectual development, either to me or to her teachers down at School #6113245. Anchored only to scores of other kids her age, they do not point to the mastery of any assigned curriculum materials, nor to the development of any particular habits of mind. They are merely invidious comparisons between my daughter and her age-mates, and they say nothing about Sarah as a learner.

School #6113245 is the Alice Fong Yu Chinese Language Immersion School. Sarah's teachers have spoken to her and her classmates in Cantonese since kindergarten. The English-language component of the curriculum has gone up from 10% to 20% of the day's activities, but Chinese language defines the school's purpose. Nothing in STAR speaks to what Alice Fong Yu has meant to Sarah — in terms of her language development, her sense of cultural difference, her sense of fitting in as a minority, her ability to look at problems from different vantage points, even her frustrations with writing complex characters in proper stroke order. STAR scores are fully reductive of all such long-term educative experiences.

And some details in STAR are ludicrous. Under "Word Study Skill," Child #008458743 answered 16 of 18 questions correctly on "Phonetic Analysis — Consonants" but only 9 of 18 questions correctly on "Phonetic Analysis — Vowels." In real life, trust me, Sarah has command of both vowels and consonants. Had she gotten as few "Consonants" questions right as she got "Vowels" questions, her overall score as a reader would have gone down into the next quartile, a negative mark not only for herself but for her school. Had she gotten as many "Vowels" questions right as she got "Consonants" questions, she would appear a truly outstanding reader and the Alice Fong Yu school that much more an outstanding inspirer of reading.

> *The California test says nothing about my daughter as a learner.*

Why the discrepancy in her vowels and consonants scores? Who knows, maybe she was tired, or just tired of being tested, or the questions were phrased differently, or she'd been taught the material differently. The salient point is the scores reflected nothing important about Sarah but only her ad hoc response to a particular test-taking situation.

However inexact, however gratuitous educationally, STAR scores have great importance in a competitive society ever less squeamish about distributing its bounties unequally. Based on these and similar scores, children will be tracked high or low, accelerated or remediated through school, win more or less impressive credentials, and land accordingly in our social hierarchy.

I resent every minute of the month (yes, an entire month) that the Alice Fong Yu school was forced to spend on preparing children for STAR and then actually administering the test. I feel a sense of uncleanliness in involving her in a travesty of pseudo-scientific measurement and covert engineering. ❏

— Jeff Zorn lives in San Francisco and teaches in the English department at Santa Clara University.

The above is reprinted from Rethinking Schools, Vol. 14, #2, Winter 1999/2000.

The Rights of Parents

The following article outlines some of the federal laws outlining parents' rights. It is reprinted from the booklet "Urgent Message for Parents" by the Center for Law and Education in Washington, D.C.

Federal laws say that parents have rights to make sure their children get what they need. The same laws that give rights to children also give them to parents.

What if your school is a Title I school?

■ Parents must plan and review the Title I program along with teachers and others.

■ How this happens must be spelled out in a plan that parents work out with the school. Parents must approve this plan.

■ You must get good information on Title I, the school, and your child's progress.

■ The school must give you training about the program. This includes how to know if your child is meeting the standards.

What if your child is covered by the Individual with Disabilities Education Act or Section 504?

■ You must be part of all decisions that are made about your child's education.

■ You must also help develop and approve your child's Individualized Education Plan (IEP).

■ You have a right to complain if you think your child is not treated fairly.

What if your child is in a vocational education program?

■ Parents and students must help plan, implement and evaluate the program.

■ They must get good information and help on what the law requires.

What if you want to speak up publicly about problems in the schools?

The first Amendment gives both parents and students that right. You also can pass out literature, join in a protest, or demonstrate peacefully.

What if you want to see your child's school records?

■ You have that right, too. The Family Educational Rights and Privacy act says the school must let you see all your child's records anywhere in the system.

■ Sometimes school staff just needs to be reminded about your rights. Start with the principal. Still, there may be times when the school won't work with you. Ask people at the district offices for help. Under Title I and other federal programs, you can appeal to state officials. They must enforce the laws on quality and standards. You also can appeal to the U.S. Department of Education.

Getting More Help

■ For more information about standards and federal funding, call the U.S. Department of Education at 1-800-USA-LEARN (1-800-872-5327).

■ To get help for children with disabilities, call the Family and Advocates Partnership for Education (FAPE) of PACER, the National Parent Information Training Center, toll-free at 1-888-248-0822. Or visit their website at www.fape.org. You can also call The National Information Center for Children and Youth with Disabilities (NICHCY) at 1-800-695-0285. Their website is www.nichcy.org

■ To find out more about your children's rights to a quality education, call the Center for Law and Education at 202-986-3000. Our website is www.cleweb.org. You can also join our Community Action for Public Schools. This is a network of parents, teachers, students, and advocates. We are working to make students' rights to quality education a reality. ❏

QUOTABLE QUOTE

"Parents must ask questions about what tests are doing to their children and their schools. They cannot simply accept the 'we're just holding the school accountable' response as satisfactory."

— *The International Reading Association, in its position statement on "High-Stakes Assessments in Reading."*

What You Can Do

BY BARBARA MINER

Parents, students, and community members are a powerful voice in the movement against test-driven reform. While by no means comprehensive, the following lists steps you can take to help replace test-driven reform with more educationally sound reform strategies.

■ Familiarize yourself with the issue. Find out what your district and state requires in terms of standardized tests, and whether these are "high-stakes" tests. This information is available from your district (ask for the department in charge of accountability or assessment). State departments of education have information on state requirements.

The websites of the national advocacy group FairTest (www. fairtest. org) and of anti-testing activist and author Alfie Kohn (www.alfiekohn .org) also have information on state standards. The Achieve web site (www.achieve.org), the official site of the corporate and gubernatorial standards movement as reflected in the National Education Summits, has nationwide data on standards and testing from a pro-testing perspective.

■ Visit your school and talk to the teachers about how standardized testing is affecting education at the school and what alternative forms of assessment might do a better job assessing your children. Share this booklet with them.

■ Talk to your children. What do they think about standardized testing? How do they think their school can be improved?

■ Link up with other parents, teachers, students, and community members concerned about standardized tests, and quality education. FairTest and Alfie Kohn's web sites have links to such groups. Other groups are also listed in the Resources section of this booklet on page 141.

■ Start your own group — perhaps as a committee of a PTA or school governance council or an independent group of concerned parents and teachers. Read this book together along with your district's and state's policies and decide on a course of action.

■ Write letters to the editors or opinion pieces

Students from Drake High School in Marin County, CA, talk to the principal while distributing leaflets in Spring 1999 opposing the state-mandated standardized test.

Marin Idenpendent Journal/Marian Little Utley

to your local newspapers, whether daily or weekly. Propose a resolution for your PTA or school council to vote on. Send it to the press. (Sample resolutions are on some of the web sites listed in the Resource section.)

■ Visit your school board members and state legislators. Speak up at public hearings on education reform.

■ Find out if your district or state allows parental opt-out of standardized tests — in other words, parents may allow their children to not take the tests, without any educational repercussions.

■ Don't give up and keep asking questions. Test-driven reform is being imposed in the name of parental and community concern about achievement. Parents, community members, and students have a powerful and unique role to play. ❐

FAILING OUR KIDS:
WHY THE TESTING CRAZE WON'T FIX OUR SCHOOLS

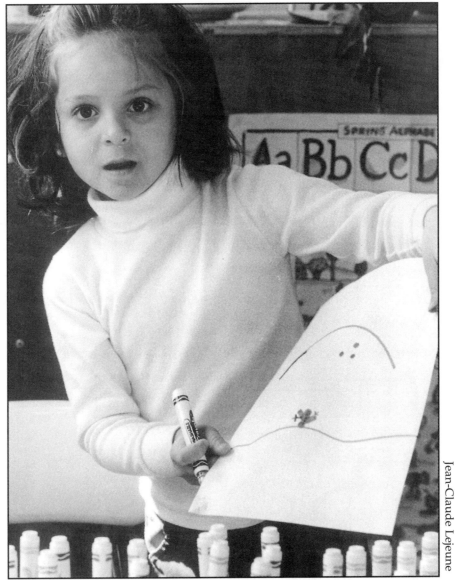

Jean-Claude Lejeune

Views From the Classroom

Dancin' Circles

Even the most rigid of state testing plans will never be able to control what every child does or thinks or writes. There may be hope.

BY DANIEL FERRI

Last March, I stood in front of my classroom and tore the plastic from a stack of papers. On those papers were printed the topic my sixth-graders, and thousands of other Illinois sixth-graders, would spend the next 40 minutes writing about.

We all are graded on the results — the students, teachers, and schools. Under state law, we all must take the Illinois Goals Assessment Program tests, the IGAPS, to ensure that across the state, all students take the same test at the same time, write about the same topic, and follow the same rules — so that everyone and everything is the same.

The IGAP is law because the easiest way for politicians to pretend they care about education is to stand up and declare that students are not learning because teachers can't teach and the schools are rotten, and we are gonna fix it by ... by taking a test. Not that those politicians have any idea what we should test for, or how we would test for it if we knew. But that does not matter. Demands for more testing sound good on TV. So the Illinois legislature told our state bureaucrats to design tests in reading, writing, math, science, and social studies, and make everyone take them for two weeks in March.

By law, Illinois students learn to write by the numbers. The first paragraph of a paper must do this this this this and this, the three main body paragraphs must do that that that that and that, and the conclusion paragraph must begin with two "thises," followed by three "thats," and end with an exciting "this."

I am not making this — or that — up.

And those are just the rules for a persuasive-type paper. We learn different rules for expository and narrative papers. There's just one problem. This is not how people write. This is how people fill out tax forms.

> There's one problem with the writing format demanded by the statewide essays. It is not how people write. It is how people fill out tax forms.

The kids hate it, especially the best writers.

"Mr. Ferri," they ask, "haven't you ever heard of foreshadowing?" "If I want to tell my story a different way, why can't I?"

I explain that our state legislature has determined that we must have standards of instruction. The children look at me like I need to blow my nose.

I tell them about basics of form that once mastered can be improvised on. They keep looking at me.

I try to convince them that these are efficient formulas for clear writing. They keep looking.

Finally I say, "Look, neither of us has any choice here. You have to take these tests, I have to give them, and some poor soul in North Carolina has to read and grade 500 of them a day. They have a list of the rules you learned for writing each kind of essay. If you don't follow a rule, they take points from your score. They don't care what you write. They only care about the rules. If you don't follow the rules, you get a bad score. The scores are published in the paper. If our scores aren't good, then people won't think our schools are good, and they won't want to move here, which will make the real estate people mad, and they will yell at the school board, who will yell at the superintendent, who will yell at the principal, who will yell at me. This is not about writing; this is about not getting yelled at."

This the kids understand.

On the day of the test, each student receives an IGAP test booklet. On the front page, students must record their name, grade, student ID number, date of birth, ethnicity, and god knows what else. Each letter or number goes in a box; under the box, with a number-2 pencil, the student must fill in a circle that corresponds to that letter or number or ethnicity. If the boxes and circles aren't filled out right, or the marks aren't dark enough, the machines can't read them, and we get yelled at.

We filled out the information pages on the day before we began the tests. After the students were finished, the pages looked as if they had been used to line bird cages. Random marks were everywhere. So my teaching partner and I stuck Post-it notes on the worst of them saying, "Print your name more clearly." Or, "Fill in circles under date of birth." Or, "Darken circles."

The morning of the first writing test my students sat vacant and resigned. I picked up the packet of prompt pages with the writing topic printed on them. I broke the plastic seal and handed them out. Then we handed out the students' test packets, some sporting Post-it reminders to "Print your name more clearly," or "Darken circles."

I stood in front of the class and read from my booklet. By law, I recited the exact same words that thousands of other sixth-grade teachers would read those mornings. "This is the test I told you about," I began. "You will have 40 minutes to" .... blah blah blah. I ended with, "Turn over the prompt page, read what the topic is, and begin writing. Good luck."

I wasn't bound by law to say good luck, but I thought it might be OK to wing it there.

The topic was, "Should students be required to wear uniforms to school?" The children picked up their pencils, took a breath, and wrote. The only sound was the turning of pages, the scratching and the sharpening of pencils.

As required by law, I announced when 20 minutes were left, then five, then when time was up. We collected the prompt pages because they must be counted and sent back to the state. We collected the test packets, and I set them on my desk while the students stretched and talked quietly. Then I heard Duane ask Becky, "What did you write about?"

"Well, I wrote about uniforms," Becky answered. "We all did, it said so on the paper."

"Mine didn't say that," Duane said. "Mine said to write about dancin' circles."

Becky and I both said, "What? What did you write about?"

"I wrote about dancin' circles," Duane

Susan Lina Ruggles

responded. "Here, I'll show you."

I reached for the pile of prompt pages, but Duane was already rummaging through the stack of test booklets. Becky said, "Those didn't say what to write about!"

"Mine did," Duane answered. He pulled his test booklet out of the stack and pointed to the Post-it stuck to the front page. On that Post-it I had written, "Darken circles."

"See, right here, it says 'Dancin' circles,'" Duane said. "So that's what I wrote about."

That morning, thousands of sixth-graders across Illinois sat at their desks, curled themselves around their pencils, stuck their tongues between their teeth, and wrote five-paragraph essays about uniforms. All, except one. His essay began, "Well, I never thought much about dancin' circles before today, but if that's what you want to

know about, well, here goes."

Somewhere in North Carolina, some poor soul will reach into the stack of 500 essays they will read that day; 499 of them will be about wearing uniforms, and one will not. I would love to watch her face when she reads it.

There may still be hope. ❏

— Daniel Ferri is a sixth-grade teacher in Lombard, IL, and is a regular commentator for Chicago Public Radio Station WBEZ, on which this essay originally aired.

This article has been reprinted in various forms in, among other places, Harper's Magazine, The National Writer's Project Newsletter, and Rethinking Schools, Vol. 13, #3, Spring 1999.

NO COMMENT

Standardized Tests and 'Outcome Bias'

Almost all standardized tests, including IQ tests and the SATs, have what is called a statistical "outcome bias" against African–Americans and other people of color. That is, African–Americans consistently score measurably lower on these tests than do White test takers. (The fact that a test has an outcome bias does not mean that the people who designed the test were consciously, or even unconsciously, biased. It simply means that there is more than an accidental difference among the scores of different groups of test takers.)

Although the gap between the scores of White and students of color has narrowed over time, it is still significant. For example, on the 1997 SAT tests, out of a possible combined score of 1600 (for verbal and math portions together), the average score for African–Americans was 857 and for Whites 1052 — a difference of 195 points.

— From the booklet No Exit? Testing, Tracking, and Students of Color in U.S. Public Schools, by the ERASE Initiative (Eliminate Racism and Advance School Equity) of the Applied Research Center in Oakland.

Ban Early Childhood Testing

A broad range of national organizations oppose standardized tests for young children. Here's why.

BY BOB PETERSON

As early as 1976 the Association for Children Education International (ACEI) called for a moratorium on standardized testing in the early school years. A decade later, it strengthened its positions, saying: "We now believe firmly that no standardized testing should occur in preschool and K-2 [kindergarten through second-grade] years. Further, we question the need to test every child in the remaining elementary years."

In 1987 the National Association for the Education of Young Children (NAEYC) adopted a policy opposing testing of kindergarten through second-grade children, ages three through eight. The NAEYC's position lists multiple cautions and points out, "Young children are not good test takers. The younger the child, the more inappropriate paper-and-pencil, large-group test administrations become."

According to Kathy Lake, Dean of Education at Milwaukee's Alverno College, some of the other professional organizations opposed to standardized testing for young children include: the National Council of Teachers of English, the National Council of Teachers of Mathematics, the National Association of Elementary School Principals, the Association for Supervision and Curriculum Development, and the National Association of Early Childhood Teacher Educators.

There are several reasons behind such nearly universal opposition. First, standardized testing of young children is neither reliable or valid. Mary Diez, Graduate Dean at Alverno College and a national expert on student assessment, argues "Everything we know about testing says that such testing is neither valid nor reliable on kids younger than third grade." According to Walt Haney of Boston College's Center for the Study of Testing, "Research clearly shows that for children below fourth grade, the mechanics of taking tests and answering on specialized answer sheets can prove more difficult than the cognitive tasks the tests are asking them to address."

> *"Testing is neither valid nor reliable on kids younger than third grade."*
>
> — *Mary Diez, Graduate Dean at Alverno College in Milwaukee.*

Bad for Morale

In addition, standardized tests are scary for young children and bad for their morale and confidence. Brenda Engel, professor of education at Lesley College in Boston, cautions that most young children are "still in the process of acquiring the complex skills involved in learning to read and write. They need a chance to consolidate these skills which, at first, are fragile and inconsistent. Premature testing, no matter how well intentioned, is discouraging to the learner — like having a work-in-progress exposed to summary judgment."

Vito Peronne, Director of Programs in Teacher Education at Harvard Graduate School of Education, argues that standardized testing of young children becomes, even though it does not provide useful information about individual children, "the basis for decisions about entry into kindergarten, promotion and retention in grades and placement in special classes; [it] leads to harmful tracking and labeling."

Peronne concludes that continuing standardized testing in the early grades "in the face of so much evidence of its deleterious effects...is the height of irresponsibility." ❐

— *Bob Peterson (repmilw@aol.com) teaches fifth grade at La Escuela Fratney in Milwaukee and is an editor of Rethinking Schools.*

The Straitjacket of Standardized Tests

*Where is the standardized test that can measure
passion for learning, respect for others, and human empathy?*

BY TOM MCKENNA

When I first met Sol Shapiro, he was in his 80's, living alone in a retirement home. He was the first person my Portland high school history class interviewed for an oral history project about our city's immigrant community, old South Portland. My students were primarily African–American. Sol was Jewish. They were young. He was old. Neither was really excited about the encounter.

We met in Sol's apartment. He was helpful as the students set up their equipment. After about 20 minutes of uncomfortable introductions, the interview began.

"My name is Sol Shapiro. I am very familiar with old South Portland." Silence. One that seemed much longer than it actually was. Quietly, almost imperceptibly, Sol began to weep. My students were stunned. They turned off the video camera and tape recorder. Soon Felicia ventured forth and placed her hand on Sol's shoulder, "It's OK, Mr. Shapiro, we understand."

Sol cleared his throat, removed his glasses, and dabbed his tears. "Thank you," he said as he looked down. "Excuse me, please, I'm very sorry." He rose from his couch and headed for a back room. My students looked at me with puzzled expressions. "What do we do now?"

We waited. After a few minutes, Sol returned. He reclaimed his seat on the couch and shared artifacts from his life with us, accompanying each with a tale from his past. Students feasted on a steady stream of photographs, letters, religious pieces, and historical documents. Much of what he shared over the next hour never got recorded on tape. Students came to class the next day with a new outlook on interviewing old people and oral history. They wanted more.

Unfortunately, given the demands of current educational reform in Oregon, teachers are finding it difficult to give students the "more" they desire.

Increasingly, teachers feel pressured to prepare students to do well on state-administered, standardized tests. We feel we have to teach to those tests; we have to "cover the content," because these tests will be the measure of our teaching and our students' learning.

A well-respected classroom veteran recently told me that "all this standardized test stuff has changed the way I teach." He wasn't comfortable with his realization. There seems to be little room any more for the use of oral history, much less time to pursue the kind of in-depth project described above. What happens if my students don't do well on the tests? What happens to my school in a district that has already "reconstituted" two others for low scores? What happens to my job in a state that recently took away teacher tenure? Those pressures are real, and I do not want to downplay them. I also want to emphasize that those pressures and the reality they reflect are the reasons why using teaching methods like oral history are so important.

Tests Can Define Teaching

Clearly, high–stakes, standardized testing, where a single multiple choice test administered out of the context of the classroom is used to ascertain both student learning and teacher effectiveness, affects much more than the way student academic performance is assessed. It also threatens to define the way teachers teach. In a world enriched with difference, the hidden curriculum of much current educational reform is singularity, sameness, and compliance.

For instance, the proposed state assessment in Oregon for social studies is a 45- to 60-question multiple-choice test to be given in the spring of students' sophomore year. Students will be held accountable for knowing discreet facts in all of the various social studies disciplines, including a survey of post Civil War U.S. history. The test is tied to state-generated standards that make no mention of race, gender, or labor. And it will be the sole

indicator of the teaching and learning in my classroom.

What score would I give students on the South Portland project? What would a multiple-choice test tell state legislators about what we all learned? Lives changed. People overcame significant historical barriers that threatened to keep them apart forever. Students were moved to social action. They came to class religiously. They sat in an orthodox synagogue with yarmulkes on their heads and learned about Judaism. They became passionate experts about urban renewal. They uncovered obscure historical documents on Saturday mornings in an Oregon History Center where they did not feel welcome.

Oral history can be a powerful classroom tool. I'm reminded of this each time I think of the South Portland video project and use oral history techniques with students. Out of necessity, students acquire and apply valuable skills in pursuit of learning that matters. They formulate questions for interviews. They work collectively to solve problems that threaten to derail hours of work. Text needs to be written and written well. It's critiqued, revised, and polished. Discovery leads to questions, and research is needed to find answers to those questions. Research leads to surprise, surprise breeds excitement, excitement spills over into passion, and students find a connection in the classroom they aren't likely to find in a more traditional setting. I know. I used to teach in a more traditional way.

Students Changed

James never missed history class. Often, he had to sneak in and out of my room to hide from the dean because he rarely attended his other classes. He was our #1 cameraman and interviewer. Jennifer uncovered a quote from a neighborhood meeting, long lost in dusty boxes, that moved her to angry tears. History came alive for her. She wove it into our collective narrative text. The words of a state official resonated when she read his comment about the people who would be moved by urban renewal: "Frankly, we don't give a damn about the renters."

The End Result

The end result of our work was a 30-minute documentary about South Portland and about the urban renewal that destroyed it. We were invited to show the piece at the Portland Art Museum auditorium. I got there early and stood outside on the street trying to help direct my students and their families to a facility where none had ever been, in a part of town where few ever ventured.

About 250 people attended our premiere that night. The students deftly answered questions from the audience and talked extensively about their experience.

Sol Shapiro was among the crowd of 250. Shortly before the show was scheduled to begin, I saw him walking toward me. He had on a plaid sports jacket with contrasting dark-blue tie and trousers. I waved. He waved back with noticeable hesitation. We greeted. "Tom, I didn't know if you would remember me."

"Sol, how could I forget?" I replied and grabbed his hand. I tried to hug him, but he pulled away.

"I need to tell you something," he said. "Before meeting your students, I was doing very little. What did I have to live for? My wife is gone, the community. But those young people reminded me I still had something to offer." I tried to interject.

"No, listen, I used to be a tailor, as you know, for years," Sol continued. "I said to myself, 'Why not share what I know with others?' So, I'm now helping out at the local community college in their fashion design program. I came here tonight to see the show and to thank your students."

We smiled. Sol gestured as if to tip his hat and made his way into the auditorium.

Students, their families, and former residents of South Portland gathered at my home for a reception after the show. Students commandeered my stereo, and their music boomed throughout my home. I went to turn it down. I stopped when I saw what was going on in my living room. Dancing hand in hand around my house were two groups of people who were about as different from each other as I could imagine and who, when I first approached them about getting together, resisted the idea. Young, old, African-American, Jewish were joined together in a celebration of each other. They celebrated a new understanding that our project helped them achieve. They embraced the differences that one time kept them apart.

Find me the standardized test that can measure the meaning of that embrace. ❐

—*Tom McKenna teaches history at a high school in Portland, OR. The names have been changed in this article, which is adapted from a story that originally appeared in The Oregonian.*

This article appeared in Rethinking Schools, Vol. 13, #3, Spring 1999.

ORGANIZATIONAL POSITION

National Council of Teachers of English

"Over the past 30 years, the National Council of Teachers of English has promulgated many resolutions opposing high-stakes testing, culminating in the 1998 resolution detailing "the limitations of standardized testing with regard to authentic assessment of the English language arts classroom" (On Testing and Equitable Treatment of Students). This resolution condemned retention based on test scores alone, the "usurpation of the English language arts curriculum" by test preparation, and testing students in English who are "not sufficiently proficient in English." Nevertheless, the intervening year has seen all of these practices escalate and in some places even enacted into law."

"NCTE joins with its sister organizations, the American Educational Research Association, American Psychological Association, and National Council on Measurement in Education in support of their Standard for Educational and Psychological Measurement 8.12, which states: "In elementary or secondary education, a decision or characterization that will have a major impact on a test taker should not automatically be made on the basis of a single test score" (1975, p. 54). Neither states, nor districts, nor schools, nor test publishers are currently abiding by this clear standard. Further, NCTE opposes single measure assessment for the initial credentialing or licensing of teachers and the continuing appointment of teachers."

— *Adopted at the 1999 NCTE annual business meeting in Denver.*

Curiouser And Curiouser

Alice's Adventure in Testingland

BY LINDA DARLING-HAMMOND

Once upon a time in Wonderland, a prestigious national commission declared that the state of health care in that country was abominable. There were so many unhealthy people walking around that the commission declared the nation at risk and called for sweeping reforms. In response, a major hospital decided to institute performance measures of patient outcomes and to tie decisions on patient dismissals as well as doctors' salaries to those measures. The most widely used instrument for assessing health in Wonderland was a simple tool that produced a single score with proved reliability. That instrument, called a thermometer, had the added advantage of being easy to administer and record. No one had to spend a great deal of time trying to decipher doctors' illegible handwriting or soliciting their subjective opinions about patient health.

Self-Serving Complaints

When the doctors discovered that their competence would be judged by how many of their patients had temperatures as measured by the thermometer as normal or below, some complained that it was not a comprehensive measure of health. Their complaints were dismissed as defensive and self-serving. The administrators, to insure that their efforts would not be subverted by recalcitrant doctors, then specified that subjective assessments of patient well-being would not be used in making decisions. Furthermore, any medicines or treatment tools not known to directly influence thermometer scores would no longer be purchased.

After a year of operating under this new system, more patients were dismissed from the hospital with temperatures at or below normal. Prescriptions of aspirin had skyrocketed, and the uses of other treatments had substantially declined. Many doctors had also left the hospital. Heart-disease and cancer specialists left in the greatest numbers, arguing obtusely that their obligation to patients required them to pay more

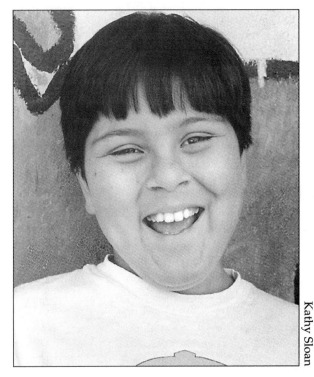

Kathy Sloan

attention to other things than to scores on the thermometer. Since thermometer scores were the only measure that could be used to ascertain patient health, there was no way to argue whether they were right or wrong.

Some years later, during the centennial Wonderland census, the census takers discovered that the population had declined dramatically and that the mortality rates had increased. As people in Wonderland were wont to do, they shook their heads and sighed, "Curiouser and curiouser." And they appointed another commission. ❐

— Linda Darling-Hammond is a professor of teaching and teacher education at Stanford University.

Reprinted with permission from the book, The Great School Debate, edited by Beatrice and Ronald Gross, published by Simon & Schuster, Inc. New York, 1985.

A longer excerpt from the book was published in Rethinking Schools, Vol. 3, #2, Winter 1988/89.

Tests from Hell

Oregon's high-stakes social studies test assumes that learning is nothing more than fact-collecting.

BY BILL BIGELOW

In late November, high school social studies teachers in the Portland area got our first look at proposed tests that the state claims will promote "higher standards." The tests — which Oregon students will need to pass in order to earn a Certificate of Initial Mastery — confirmed our worst fears. They are a collection of random multiple choice questions, demanding rote memorization and the application of almost no higher level thinking skills. If anything resembling these pilot tests is implemented, social studies teachers will have to substantially dumb-down our curriculum to insure students' success.

The problem with the tests is not any particular question. Their essential wrong-headedness lies with the assumption that learning is nothing more than fact-collecting. Test questions lurch from the Constitution to the New Deal to global climate to rivers in Africa to hypothetical population projections and back to World War One. Each of seven pilot tests in circulation has about 50 questions but, given the randomness of the topics, there could be an almost infinite number of other facts that could be sought on future versions.

> *The tests' essential wrong-headedness lies with the assumption that learning is nothing more than fact-collecting.*

What Is a Teacher to Do?

What's a conscientious teacher to do? There is no way to adequately prepare students for these tests without turning our classrooms into vast wading pools of information for students to memorize without critical reflection. Teachers will have to reorient our curricula away from the role plays, simulations, research projects, essay writing, and other in-depth activities that breathe life into social studies and allow students to probe beneath the surface of "the facts."

Students can know a great deal about a subject and yet do poorly on the new tests. For example, one question asks which Constitutional Amendment gave women the right to vote. But the test asks almost nothing else about the movement that resulted in that Amendment. Last year, my U.S. History students at Franklin performed a role play on the 1848 Seneca Falls, NY women's rights conference, the first formal U.S. gathering to demand greater equality for women, including the right to vote. Several students researched and wrote detailed papers on feminist activists like Elizabeth Cady Stanton, the Grimke sisters, and Susan B. Anthony. They knew a lot about the long struggle for women's rights. However, unless they could recall that one isolated fact — that it was the 19th and not the 16th, 17th or 18th Amendment (the other test choices) that gave women the vote — the state of Oregon would have considered all their extensive knowledge irrelevant. How does this state-mandated memory contest promote "higher standards"?

In a demonstration of its own shaky grasp of the material on which it tests students, the state shows that the reverse is true as well: one can master isolated morsels of fact and remain ignorant about the issues that give those facts meaning. For example, in a test question repeated throughout the seven pilot tests, the state uses the term "suffragette," an inappropriate and dismissive substitute for "suffragist." Someone who had actually studied the movement would know this. As Sherna Gluck points out in *From Parlor to Prison*, women in the suffrage movement considered this diminutive term "an insult when applied to them by most of the American press."

Inevitably, the state's "one best answer" approach vastly oversimplifies and misrepresents complex social processes. One question reads: "In 1919, over 4.1 million Americans belonged to labor unions. By 1928, that number had dropped to 3.4 million. Which of the following best accounts for that drop?" I presume the correct answer is A: "Wages increased dramatically, so workers did not need unions." All the other answers are o b v i o u s l y wrong, but is this answer "correct"? Do workers automatically leave unions when they secure higher wages? Weren't mechanization and scientific management factors in undermining traditional craft unions? Did the post-World War "Red Scare," with systematic attacks on radical unions like the Industrial

Workers of the World and deportations of foreign-born labor organizers affect union membership? The state would reward students for selecting an historical soundbite that is as shallow as it is wrong.

Gaps in Curriculum

And I wonder if Oregon parents know that the state standards, on which the new tests are allegedly based, remove huge areas from the high school curriculum: virtually nothing before the last decade or so of the 19th century is supposed to be covered in high school. No early European/Native American contacts, no American Revolution, no slavery or slave resistance, no Abolition Movement, no Civil War, no building of the railroads, no Reconstruction. The pilot tests include not a single question on any of these topics so vital to understanding today's society. Evidently, the state supposes that the earlier something happened, the less complex it is; thus, it should be studied only by younger children.

In meetings with Portland area social studies teachers, Oregon Department of Education officials acknowledge that the tests are superficial and that other more thoughtful assessments would be preferable. But "the public" demands tests, they claim, and it would take several more years to develop something better.

Parents and "the public" do not want tests

that are little more than "high stakes Trivial Pursuit or Jeopardy," in the words of one scholar. This is my twenty-first year as a Portland teacher. My contact with parents leads me to believe that they want their kids to think deeply and clearly, to write with knowledge and passion. Parents want their children to know that they can make a difference in the world. They want them to be engaged in classroom activities that draw on their youthful energies and challenge them to question. I've never had a parent tell me: "Get my child to memorize as many facts as possible."

The Oregon Department of Education is about to inaugurate tests that will hurt education. Instead, it should support Oregon teachers as we work at the grassroots level to develop genuinely higher standards for students. It can help us develop assessments that are integrated into the curriculum, that are not overly prescriptive, and that promote complex thinking. It is not too late for the Oregon Department of Education to put the brakes on its 50-fact tests. ❒

— Bill Bigelow (bbpdx@aol.com) is an editor of Rethinking Schools and teaches at Franklin High School in Portland, OR.

This article originally appeared in The Oregonian and is reprinted with permission of the author.

The article also appeared in Rethinking Schools, Vol. 13, #3, Spring 1999.

'High-Stakes' Harm

How can teachers maintain their critical stance toward assessment, yet still help prepare students to take 'high-stakes' tests?

BY LINDA CHRISTENSEN

While critical teachers might stand back and say we don't want to have anything to do with tests, we can't just go on with business as usual. The question for anyone who cares about kids is: How do we retain our critical stance on assessments while preparing students for them? Can we "teach the tests" without compromising what we know to be true about teaching and learning?

My friends at low-achieving elementary schools have been counseled to acclimate students to tests by redesigning their regular curriculum so that students can get accustomed to multiple choice questions. But in a classroom sensitive to equity issues, that's not easy. How can a role play about an important historical or social issue be reformatted into a multiple choice activity? How does an a, b, c, d answer format encourage students to look at issues from the perspective of an interned Japanese American or a Cherokee Indian facing government-ordered removal?

To achieve real gains in student knowledge and skill, we must continue to give students a rich curriculum with varied opportunities to use their learning in real world activities. However, I live in a state that has filled our classrooms with tests. I believe we must seize the opening to demystify the tests — to help our students critically analyze these exams and the assumptions behind them — as well as motivate them and coach them in test-taking skills so they may potentially be able to increase their performance.

Questioning Assumptions

A social justice curriculum equips students to question what is often taken for granted. Tests have become as much a part of the curriculum as books. (In fact, these days there seems to be more money for testing, test preparation, and test scor-

> *We must demystify the tests — analyze the exams and their assumptions — as well as coach students in test-taking skills.*

ing than for the books we need to teach. A good question might be, "Why are we spending so much money on testing when we need books?") In critical classrooms, we can make testing the object of our curiosity.

Begin by questioning the origins and purpose of these tests. Some of the questions one might ask students: Who made the tests? What are the tests supposed to measure? How will the test scores be used? For example, in Oregon, students take multiple tests. One might think that these tests will be used to help teachers more accurately assess their students' abilities or progress to improve instruction. But because the tests are given during the school year — from February to April — and the scores aren't returned to the schools until the school year has almost ended, one has to question the legitimacy of that claim.

Another way to scrutinize the tests is to find statistics generated from these exams. In my school district, the local newspaper happily prints scores and rates schools, but our research and evaluation department also has broken the scores down by gender and race. Have students examine the statistics. Which school in the district usually receives high scores? Which ones don't? Is there a pattern? Are the scores related to parents' income? Race?

This one is tricky because you don't want to leave the students with the idea that race or income are indicators of intelligence or the only factors determining academic achievement. It is important to examine the questions to see how the content might favor one race or one gender or one income bracket. *FairTest Examiner* is a good resource for this information on the SATs.

Sometimes you can find these selections in your own city or state assessments. Ruthann Hartley, a former colleague from Jefferson High School, was furious after she administered the state reading test last year. According to Hartley, a disproportionate number of questions examined a passage and chart from Consumer Reports on frequent flyer benefits. Hartley noted, "This is a problematic item for teenagers, but especially for low-income students who don't travel. Passages like this raise the question of what is being tested. If students answer incorrectly, is it because they can't read or because they don't have the background knowledge?"

Students might also question how the test results are used. Who benefits if they get high scores? Are students placed in honors or remedial classes? Given scholarships? Special programs? Are teachers' or principals' salaries tied to the results? Have students interview school and district administrators and department chairs about how students are placed in honors classes, talented and gifted programs. Are test scores the only criterion?

Asking students to become investigators prior to exam time can help put the tests in a social context, but more than that, it diminishes the size of their opponent. Students see behind the Wizard of Oz curtain and realize that no geniuses are laboring to construct these tests.

SAT Origins

While my junior and senior students weren't saddled with the Certificate of Initial Mastery (CIM) reading, writing, and math tests that Oregon 3rd-, 5th-, 8th-, and 10th-graders currently take, my students were having their behinds kicked by the SATs. After their encounters with

Jean-Claude Lejeune

these grueling tests, they fumed to me and their math teachers. "Those tests might as well have been written in Greek!" Shameka said after her Saturday was ruined by the exams. For my students, an investigation of the history of the SATs was as critical as teaching them how to improve their scores. The SAT/ACT scores become a brand of shame students carry long after they bubble in the last answer. If they score low on the test, they doubt themselves and wonder if they are as capable as the kid who scored higher.

To help students understand the origins of the exam and help them put the scores in perspective, my class reads a chapter from David Owens' book *None of the Above* called "The Cult of Mental Measurement." In this essay, Owens describes the racist past of the SATs and also points out how race continues to be a factor in these kinds of standardized tests today. Students are outraged by their discoveries. (For example, the founder of the SATs, Carl Campbell Brigham, published in the same

Jean-Claude Lejeune

eugenics journal that Adolf Hitler wrote for.) But even without this gem of a chapter to use, getting students to investigate the origin and use of tests in their school district or state is a good place to start. (See Bill Bigelow's "Testing, Tracking, and Toeing the Line: A Role Play on the Origins of the Modern High School" in *Rethinking Our Classrooms*, published by Rethinking Schools.

Examining the Tests

Once students have gained a critical edge on the tests, we might be able to help them improve their performance by examining both the content and the format of the tests themselves. The more they know about how the questions are put together as well as the vocabulary of the material, the better prepared they are to meet the challenge.

In my senior English class, students demystified the SATs and used their knowledge to teach others about their discoveries. We started by analyzing each of the verbal sections of the SATs. We examined the instructions, language, and "objectives" of each section. We took apart the analogies and figured out the kinds of relationships they

> *I ask my students, "Who benefits from these tests?"*

paired. (We used The Princeton Review: Cracking the SAT to help us wade through and prepare. David Owens wrote the foreword.) We looked at how the language and culture of the SATs reflected the world of upper class society with words like heirloom, inheritance, conservatory, regatta.

After examining each section and taking the tests a few times, I asked students to construct their own tests using the culture, content and vocabulary of our school—from sports to dance to awards. Pairs of students worked together developing questions which the entire class examined, then we put together the JAT, Jefferson Achievement Tests. Following are two selections from the JAT.

The Jefferson Achievement Tests

Each question below consists of a related pair of words or phrases, followed by four lettered pairs of words or phrases. Select the lettered pair that best expresses a relationship similar to that expressed in the original pair.

1. Tony: Play:

a) Broadway : Annie
b) Oscar : Tom Hanks
c) Brandon : soccer
d) Howard Cherry : sports

(The "correct answer is d. The "Tony" is an award given for a play. At Jefferson the "Howard Cherry" is an award given for sports.)

2. New Growth : Perm:
a) press : straight
b) weave : long
c) corn row : braid
d) nails : fill

(The correct answer is d. When you get "new growth" it is time for a perm. In the same way, if you wear acrylic nails and your nails grow out, you need to get a fill.)

After completing the test, students took the JAT up to Ruth Hubbard's education classes at Lewis and Clark College. My students asked the pre-service teachers to imagine that the JAT was a high-stakes test that will determine their future—what college they get into, scholarships, etc. After the tests, students discussed the issues of testing and language.

Developing their own analogies from Jefferson's culture helped students understand the mechanics of the exam. It also made them see that if they were the test makers, using their culture and their vocabulary, they could also devise a test that could be used to exclude some and include others.

Perhaps the most important lesson of the unit came when students asked, "Why would someone want to devise a test to keep students out of a college they want to enter?"

Teaching students to examine the history and motives of local and state tests and preparing them for the big day(s), is no substitute for fighting to end the encroachment of assessments in our classrooms. Nor is it a substitute for day-in, day-out teaching that encourages real-life thinking and learning. The work I've proposed may demystify the tests and help students question their legitimacy. Our bigger work as teachers and parents is to engage in the battle to stop testing that makes young people question their ability. ❐

— Linda Christensen is a Rethinking Schools editor and Language Arts Coordinator for Portland (OR) Public Schools.

The above is excerpted from Rethinking Schools, Vol. 13, #3, Spring 1999.

NO COMMENT

Texas Tests Discriminate

Eighty-five percent of those who do not pass the [Texas Assessment of Academic Skills] test are either African–American or Latino. Although minority test scores have gone up since the TAAS was first administered, this is hardly heartening for several reasons, since the test administration also correlates to a higher dropout rate and to higher retention rates.

One study estimates that between 20 and 25 percent of Mexican–Americans who do make it to the end of tenth grade drop out, in great part because of the test. According to one Texas Education Association report, Whites have a 72% greater chance of progressing to the 12th grade without ever being retained. This contrasts markedly with the probabilities of 46 and 44% for African–Americans and Latinos, respectively."

— Angela Valenzuela, faculty member at the University of Texas at Austin and author of Subtractive Schooling: U.S. Mexican Youth and the Politics of Caring. Valenzuela made the comments during an on-line forum in the summer of 2000 sponsored by the Harvard Education Letter.

Teaching About Testing

Suggestions on how teachers can use this booklet and other resources to help students think critically about standardized tests.

BY BILL BIGELOW

When students are not encouraged to think critically about tests, they are more likely to internalize the judgments of those tests as legitimate. The consequences — for example, placement in a particular "ability" group or being awarded or denied promotion to the next grade level — may appear fair or even scientific. No matter how culturally biased, curricularly invalid, or just downright dumb the tests are, students can end up blaming themselves for poor performance.

It's vital that teachers, parents and policymakers think clearly about the history and effects of standardized testing. But we also need to engage students themselves in a critical inquiry. After all, they are the ones most directly affected by the testing craze. Below are a few curriculum suggestions and resources on testing issues. As indicated, many of the articles in this special publication may be used effectively with students.

■ The country's first testing craze occurred early in the 20th century. It was unfair and discriminatory — just like today's testing craze. See "Testing, Tracking, and Toeing the Line," for a role play that shows students first-hand how and why standardized testing and tracking began in the United States (pp. 117-124, in *Rethinking Our Classrooms*, Volume I). Included in the role play is a 1920 "mental ability test" developed by Stanford University, an excellent classroom resource for students to critique.

■ Follow the role play with chapter nine, "The Cult of Mental Measurement," from David Owens' book, *None of the Above*. It is a bit difficult, but prompts students to think critically about the meritocratic rationale of the first Scholastic Aptitude Test and provides some startling background about the individuals who developed them, one of whom wrote for the same eugenics journal that reprinted Hitler's "Text of the German Sterilization Statute." See Linda Christensen's article, "Writing the Word and the World," in her book,

Reading, Writing, and Rising Up, for how to use dialogue journals with Owens' chapter. Also see her article in this volume, "High Stakes Harm" (p. 48), that describes how her students wrote an "achievement test" based on the culture of her school and then administered it to college students. This activity — one that other teachers could replicate — helps students understand how cultural bias may be manifested in test questions.

■ Alan Stoskopf's article, "The Forgotten History of Eugenics" (p. 76), is a fine overview of the racist origins of today's high stakes testing. Students could list the social conditions that precipitated the first eugenics movement and decide which similar features exist in today's society.

■ Ask students to write about their own recent testing experiences. Encourage them to tell these as stories and then offer an opportunity for students to read these to one another. As they listen, ask them to notice themes that recur in each other's writing. Talk about what they noticed. Follow these by sharing the student-written pieces from this volume: "'No' is the Right Answer" (p. 26), and "Students Say 'Enough'" (p. 30). How do the observations in these articles compare to students' stories and discussions? (These might be better used when considering how students should respond to the current wave of high stakes testing.) Miriam Cohen's book, *First Grade Takes a Test* (Bantam Doubleday Dell, 1980) is a delightful illustrated story about the impossibility of measuring children's knowledge with standardized tests. It could be used with students of all ages and would provide an excellent prompt as they write their own testing stories.

■ Students who participate in the "Testing, Tracking, and Toeing the Line" role play and read David Owens' chapter or Alan Stoskopf's article will recognize the racist origins of standardized testing. Is standardized testing still racist? Read with students Derrick Z. Jackson's article, "At Best, Silly, At Worst, Racist" (p. 18). What evidence does

ANIMAL TESTING

List at least four ingredients of slop.

Where is the best place to throw up hair balls?
☐ A rug
☐ The bed
☐ A sweater
☐ The radiator

Should you chase a ball into the street?
☐ Yes
☐ No
☐ You do what you have to do.

Write a brief reaction to this statement: Farmer McGregor is essentially a decent man.

KOPF ©1997

L.I. Kopf

Jackson provide to support his thesis? What other evidence supports or contradicts his thesis? Makani Themba-Nixon's article, "High-Stakes Testing Slights Multiculturalism" (p. 32), is also an accessible and concrete story about the discriminatory way that standards and tests drive the curriculum.

■ What kind of teaching and learning does testing push aside? Have students read Tom McKenna's article, "The Straitjacket of Standardized Tests" (p. 42). McKenna describes an important oral history project that is incompatible with the new testing regime in his state. Brainstorm and list with students all the important kinds of knowledge not easily assessed by standardized tests. If one effect of high stakes testing is increased "teaching to the test," then this knowledge will be less emphasized during the present testing craze.

■ How should students respond to the testing craze? Ask students to list and discuss all the possible ways they can imagine that students might respond to the tests. Ask your classes to read some of the articles in this volume on parent and student perspectives: "We Object" (p. 33), by parents of Massachusetts fourth-grade students; "'No' Is the Right Answer" (p. 26); "Students Say 'Enough'" (p. 30); and "MCAS Test Draws Fire" (p. 24). Ask them how the positions expressed in

these articles compare with their thoughts on how to respond to the tests.

■ Have your students conduct an "alternative assessment" of the school community by using the questions included in "Their Report Card — and Ours" (p. 106), suggested by members of Portland Area Rethinking Schools (PARS). Divide students into five groups corresponding to the headings in the PARS "report card": Curriculum, Student Assessment, Equity for All Students, Health and Safety, and Parents and Community in the Life of the School. Make sure they understand each of the questions, then ask the groups to assess their school. When they encounter a question they don't know the answer to, encourage them to decide how they might find one. Brainstorm with students how they could take action based on their answers to the "report card" questions?

■ The title of Tom McKenna's article is a metaphor: standardized tests are straitjackets. Ask students to think of other metaphors for standardized tests or the testing craze. They should keep in mind what they've learned about the history of testing and resistance to testing. List their ideas on the board or overhead. Give students paper and colored pens and ask them to make metaphorical drawings that illustrate their impressions.

— Bill Bigelow (bbpdx@aol.com) is an editor of Rethinking Schools and teaches at Franklin High in Portland, OR.

One Size Fits Few

Do the people developing state standards have any clue about kids — and why it may not be a great idea to force Moby Dick down the throats of 15-year-olds?

BY SUSAN OHANIAN

Standardistos in most of the 50 states are high on skills amphetamines, engaged in what amounts to a standards arms race. These days, every Standardisto is looking for 10 minutes of fame, proving "my standards are tougher than your standards."

If John Silber, [former] chairman of the Massachusetts State Board of Education, has his way, students will read from a core list, including Milton's sonnets and Moby Dick. Now you know and I know that anyone who says high-schoolers should read Moby Dick:

- Doesn't know any fifteen-year-olds,
- Has never read Moby Dick,
- Has read Moby Dick, has a fifteen-year-old in the house, and wants to get even.

I worry that a whole lot of the Standardistos' curriculum exists on this "get even" premise. I suffered, so why should today's kids get a break? The sad thing is that Moby Dick is a great book. It wasn't until I was 42 years old that I'd sufficiently recovered from my college experience to try it again. Okay, I confess: At 42, I still skipped the rope-tying stuff. It just seems a pity that in the name of Standards, we ruin so many wonderful books by forcing them prematurely on kids.

> *California's standards for fifth graders read like the outline for half a dozen fat college texts.*

California's Standards

Sometime back, a number of blue-ribbon commissions expressed concern that American kids were getting too little history. Now California produces a document showing us how to give them too much.

Here's paragraph three:

"The standards serve as the basis for statewide assessments, curriculum frameworks and instructional materials, but methods of instructional delivery remain the responsibility of local educators."

Right. As representatives of the state, the Standardistos get to decide what will be taught, the texts used to teach it, and the tests taken to make sure it was taught. "Local educators" are left to provide "instructional delivery." Thus, the avowed purpose of the Standardistos is to obliterate teaching.

Plenty of people denounced the National History Standards for not teaching appreciation of the Constitution, so the California Standardistos make sure California Kids will have the Constitution coming out of the kazoo.

Just when you think it might be safe to go out at night, here comes 1.6 of the California History/Social Science Standards:

"Students understand basic economic concepts and the role of individual choice in a free-market economy, in terms of:

- The concept of exchange and the use of money to purchase goods and services.
- The specialized work that people do to manufacture, transport, and market goods and services and the contribution of those who work in the home."

Remember, this is Grade One. Second graders label a map of North America from memory: Countries, oceans, Great Lakes, major rivers, mountain ranges. Second-graders also read the biographies and "explain how heroes from long ago and the recent past make a difference in others' lives." The Standardistos suggest: George Washington Carver, Marie Curie, Louis Pasteur, Albert Einstein, Indira Gandhi, Abraham Lincoln, Jackie Robinson. I sense E. D. Hirsch's influence here. The peculiarity of the grouping as well as its developmental inappropriateness has that Hirschian feel to it.

Fourth graders get latitude and longitude and the Spanish missions. Many California teachers won't see much new here. I remember studying the Spanish missions in fourth grade eons ago. Of

HEY KID, I JUST SET THE STANDARDS, I DON'T CARE HOW YOU REACH THEM!

course, the text then, like the text today, does not talk about Father Serra's missions as a system of forced labor.

In the new California standards, fifth graders "describe the entrepreneurial characteristics" of early explorers such as Columbus and Coronado. They also "understand the purpose of the state constitution, its key principles, and its relationship to the U.S. Constitution (with an emphasis on California's Constitution.)" Actually, I, a native Californian, have vague memories of learning — no, memorizing — all that California Constitution stuff. I wonder today, how much poorer a life I lead for not remembering a bit of it for longer than six minutes after regurgitating the facts on a test. All I remember is the bear on the flag.

There is more matter here than I can possibly describe. This document reads like the outline for at least half a dozen fat college texts. One thing that catches my eye is that fifth graders are expected to understand the course and consequence of the American Revolution, in terms of "identifying and mapping the major military battles, campaigns and turning points of the Revolutionary War, the roles of American and British leaders, and the Indian leader alliances on both sides."

Standard 7.9, for seventh graders, is the penultimate standard. As fifth graders, students had to learn the history of civilization in medieval times. Now, under 7.9, they will analyze the historical developments of the Reformation, in terms of:

■ The causes for the internal decay of the Catholic church (e.g., tax policies, selling of indulgences),

■ The theological, political, and economic ideas of the major figures during the Reformation (e.g., Erasmus, Martin Luther, John Calvin, William Tindale),

■ The influence of new practices of church self-government among Protestants on the development of democratic practices and ideas of federalism,

■ The location and identification of European regions that remained Catholic and those that became Protestant and how the division affected the distribution of religions in the New World,

■ How the Counter-Reformation revitalized the Catholic Church and the forces that propelled the movement (e.g., St. Ignatius of Loyola and the Jesuits, the Council of Trent),

■ The institution and impact of missionaries on Christianity and the diffusion of Christianity from Europe to other parts of the world in the early modern period, including their location on a world map,

■ The "Golden Age" of cooperation between Jew and Muslims in Medieval Spain which promoted creativity in art, literature, and science, including how it was terminated by the religious persecution of individuals and groups (e.g., the Spanish Inquisition and the expulsion of Jews and Muslims from Spain in 1492).

Seventh graders meet John Calvin! William Tindale! The Council of Trent! The prospect leaves me breathless. Surely a person must be unusually dense to think seventh graders can be forced to drink of this brew. I confess I thought it wonderfully apt that William Tindale is of such secondary significance that he isn't even in my Merriam Webster's Collegiate Dictionary: Tenth Edition. But I kept checking and discovered that he's there. Standardistos, ever esoteric, employ the third-alternate spelling.

Seeking Asylum for Seventh Graders

Time out. Does anybody out there know any seventh graders? As a refresher course, let's hear from premier New Hampshire middle school teacher Linda Rief. This description of emerging adolescence as both the best of times and the worst of times is from her book, *Seeking Diversity: Language Arts with Adolescents* (Heinemann, 1992):

Marilyn Nolt

Working with teenagers is not easy. It takes patience, humor, and love. Yes, love of kids who burp and fart their way through eighth grade. Who tell you "Life sucks!" and everything they do is "Boring!" Who literally roll to the floor in hysterical laughter when you separate the prefix and the suffix from the word "prediction" and ask them for the root and what it means. Who wear short, skin-tight skirts and leg-laced sandals, but carry teddy bears in their arms. Who use a paper clip to tattoo Jim Morrison's picture on their arm during quiet study, while defending the merits of Tigger's personality in Winnie-the-Pooh. Who send obscene notes that would make a football player blush, written in pink marker, blasting each other for stealing or not stealing a boyfriend, and sign the note "Love, _____ P. S. Please write back."

No one who knows seventh graders would insist that the subject matter will take precedence for longer than about 12 minutes a period; that's on good days. "Bad-mannered little shits" is a phrase that seventh-grade teachers understand. It was coined by Noel Coward, referring, not to seventh graders, but to the Beatles.

QUOTABLE QUOTE

"I believe standardization will make it harder to hold people accountable and harder to develop sound and useful standards. The intellectual demands of the 21st Century, as well as the demands of democratic life, are best met by preserving plural definitions of a good education, local decision-making, and respect for ordinary human judgments."

— *Educator Deborah Meier in her book, Will Standards Save Public Education?*

The above is just one of 11 standards that California Standardistos say seventh graders will master in their history classes. If I were a parent in California, I would be looking for a transfer out-of-state rather than face the savage reality of the homework these standards will generate. A class-action lawsuit against the Board of Education might be another possibility.

An interesting footnote: No history/social studies standards have been written for ninth graders in California "in deference to current California practice in which grade nine is the year students traditionally choose a history/social studies elective." I have read all the standards documents, including the minutes of commission meetings, produced by the California Standardistos. In twelve grades on imperatives and explications, this is the only mention of students getting a choice.

California Standardistos were very conscious that these are the first-ever statewide academic standards for history. In announcing the California Academic Commission's approval of its standards, History/Social Science Committee Chair Lawrence Siskind said, "Our History/Social Science Standards are balanced and academically rigorous. I am especially proud of the civic values and virtues which they impart. When they graduate high school, California students will be ready to vote, to serve on juries, and to take their place in society as responsible citizens. Should they ever be called upon to fight for their country, these standards will teach them why their country is worth fighting for."

No comment. ❑

Marilyn Nolt

— This article is exerpted and condensed from Chapter 5, "Californication," of One Size Fits Few: The Folly of Educational Standards, by Susan Ohanian (Portsmouth, NH: Heinemann, 1999). To order call: 1-800-225-5800.

Testing and Students With Disabilities

Following are general principles regarding standards and testing of students with disabilities. The guidelines were developed by Kathleen Boundy of the Center for Law and Education, a nationwide advocacy group.

One of the issues that often comes up is the effect that accountability measures have on students with disabilities.

The legal framework rests on federal legislation known as the Individuals with Disabilities Education Act (IDEA) resolution, with amendments in 1997, and Section 504 of the Rehabilitation Act of 1973, the civil rights statute barring discrimination against persons with disabilities. Compliance with the federal legislation is due, in part, to how well a district provides the resources and staff training necessary to adequately serve all students with disabilities.

■ Assessments that are valuable for all students will generally be valuable for students with disabilities. Likewise, educational practices that can be harmful to all students, such as "high-stakes" tests , are also a disservice to students with disabilities.

■ Students with disabilities have the right to a high quality, free and appropriate public education that is consistent with state educational standards set for all other students.

■ Each student's Individualized Education Program (IEP), which outlines the student's educational goals and how those goals will be met, should be used as a tool for achieving the standards set for all.

■ Given the poor history of ensuring that students with disabilities participate in the general curriculum and receive the content provided all other children, it is essential they be included in any stan-

> *Students with disabilities must be given the instruction necessary to make progress toward the educational goals set for all children.*

dards-based education reform initiatives.

■ Students with disabilities must be provided the curriculum and instruction necessary to allow them to make meaningful progress toward meeting the standards set for all children. Many children with severe disabilities, including cognitive disabilities, are able to participate in at least portions of the general curriculum, when specialized instruction, supplementary aids, and related services are provided.

Include All Students

■ State and district assessments and accountability measures must include all students, regardless of the nature or severity of the disability. Indeed, most students with disabilities can participate in large-scale assessments, in whole or in part, if provided accommodations or other test modifications (such as having a non-reading test read to a student if their disabilities affect reading; or modifying the time limit on the test.) Such accommodations and modifications, as necessary, are required by federal law. The use of accommodations and modifications are to be determined by a student's IEP team.

■ Sometimes accommodations are not enough for some students to participate in the state or district wide assessment. Students who could demonstrate progress toward meeting the standards, if assessed differently, must be provided that opportunity. These students might be assessed using a performance assessment. For example, a student who cannot demonstrate his or her actual level of proficiency or mastery of particular standards by using the written standardized test instrument (even with accommodations or modifications) but who could do so by building a model or using a computer program, must arguably be provided such an alternative.

■ On the other hand, an alternate assessment measuring different content may be needed for the limited population of students with such severe cognitive disabilities that they are unable to demonstrate any measurable progress toward meeting even the broadest, most basic standards using a standardized assessment or an alternative assessment.

■ If states and districts considered and addressed the educational needs of all students, including those with severe cognitive disabilities, when establishing standards for all children, there should be very few instances when it would be necessary to use an alternate assessment that measures different content. ❑

— *For more information, contact the Center for Law and Education at 617-451-0855 or online at www.cleweb.org.*

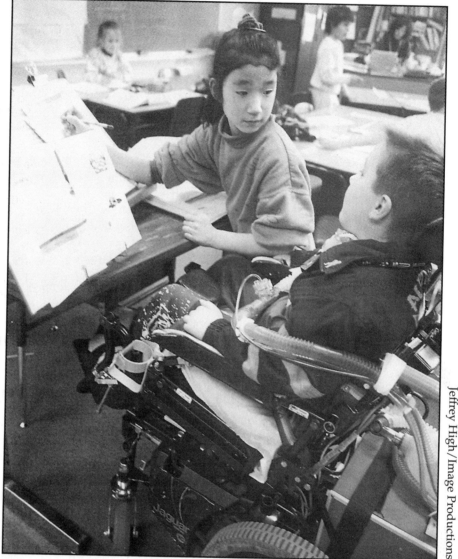

Jeffrey High/Image Productions

NO COMMENT

State Scholarships Tied to Tests

In Michigan, students who do well on the state's tests receive scholarships of $2,500.

A number of people are disturbed about the inequities built into such a system of rewards. A study of 1998 MAP scores, for instance, found that while 36% of White students would have qualified for the scholarhip that year, only 7% of African-American students and 23% of Latino students would have qualified, according to the Winter 2000 issue of the FairTest *Examiner*.

Michigan allows students, with parent permission, to opt out of the state's testing. The scholarship policy was developed after a statewide test boycott resulted in a participation rate as low as 5% in some Michigan districts.

A Grim Fairy Tale

*How the fog of test-driven boredom
came to dull children's minds and dim their senses.*

BY CYNTHIA ELLWOOD AND DAVID LEVINE

Once upon a time in a great kingdom on a great lake, a tremendous clamor arose among the people. "Our schools," they cried, "are not making the grade! Our children learn little; they cannot even write." And so the King's High Council on Schools convened in the castle's Grand Hall to hear the views of the populace. The millers and masons and candlestick-makers said their children learned less than those outside the city walls (and they had statistics to prove it). The merchants complained bitterly that so-called graduates could not compose the simplest of business letters. And for once, the Representatives of the Common People agreed with the merchants. "Our schools must be held to objective and effective standards!" they vehemently asserted. Even the High Lord of Schools, the Earl of McMuffin, submitted that the time had come for change.

The King's Council, quite unable to remember a time when the people were so vocal and united, bowed their heads and whispered urgently among themselves. Soon enough, the buglers sounded their horns, the town criers sucked in deep breaths, and there was issued a Grand Proclamation of the King's High Council on Schools:

"Hear Ye! Hear Ye!" cried the criers. "Let it be known throughout the length and breadth of the Kingdom of Greats that no child shall graduate from the Higher School ere he can compose an essay of five paragraphs and a business letter that doth meet fine standards of formality. Furthermore, let no child sally forth with a diploma who hath not first mastered the rules of our Great Language—the ins and outs, the twists and turns, the apostrophes and the semi-colons, the capitals and the quotation marks. Let our children prove they

can separate the terse from the interminable, the apt from the inappropriate, and the language of the low and vulgar from the dialect of the Great and Standard! Then indeed shall greatness ring throughout the land!"

And so began the Era of the Competency Examination, and (though some children complained) most everyone was gladdened.

In the classrooms there was such a frenzy! Most conscientiously did the schoolmasters drill their young charges, and most heartily did they chastise the youths for mixing up their homonyms or capitalizing their seasons. The worksheets flew like snow flurries, and the youngsters penned five-part theme after five-part theme. They wrote of the three things they would do with a million gold coins, their three most favored summer activities, three things to do at the waterfront, three ways to make winter less miserable, three ways to plow a field, and three ways to arise in the morning. They duly framed each theme with an introduction and a conclusion. Most mastered their threes and fives, but there were slow learners. Tom the Tinker's Son, having been asked to discuss his three favored pastimes, could think of only one: playing with his falcon, Franklin. He told how Franklin dipped and soared, and how quickly Franklin learned. Tom stated with conviction that a bird could love a boy, and he confided he had sometimes longed to be himself a falcon, sweeping over the kingdom and frolicking in the winds.

To which his master replied, "Where is your five-part form? Alas, such run-ons! Your spelling is improving!"

Tom finally learned the right rote to write. He discovered that one could write by recipe, finding a thought to fit each slot. After all, as his schoolmaster earnestly advised, there would be time after the exam to write with beauty and inspiration. But a curious thing did come about. After the exam (and he did pass), no desire to write remained in Tom. "Too boring," he said.

Indeed, the fog of boredom crept into each classroom and hung lazily there, dulling minds and dimming the senses. In few classrooms did master and students pause to wonder at the power of language, to savor the sounds, or to play

Tom finally learned the right rote to write. He discovered that one could write by recipe, finding a thought to fit each slot.

with rhythm and meaning. In few classrooms did the Higher Schoolers ever read whole books, entering into fantasy to better grasp the real.

As they toiled over letters, worksheets, and five-part themes, there was no time to read, question, probe, debate, and write about the issues which engaged their passions and their minds.

And curiously, those who dutifully passed the tests still struggled at the University, still lacked for jobs, still compared poorly with the children from outside the city walls.

So the people came together to ponder upon the problem. One wise old man said, "Keep the test — but cast out that frozen five-paragraph formula, lest tests should provoke the mind and teach our youth that good writing means thinking hard about things that matter and expressing those thoughts well." A sage old woman, equally esteemed, declared that there should be no tests that punished the victims but other ways to better the schools from the kindergarten forward. A brave knight and slayer of dragons elocuting eloquently averred that the problems went beyond the schools to the bedrock of the kingdom; it would require all the people working everywhere to make the needed changes. And though they found no single magic answer, the people agreed that such a great kingdom needed solutions greater and more thoughtful than what had yet been tried.

When all had been said and vigorously debated, young Tom Tinker was appointed to write a report, so that all the kingdom might hear the concerns of the citizenry there gathered. Tom worked mightily at the report, for these ideas were important (and passionately felt). He saw quite clearly how problems interlocked. But try as he might, our poor young Tom could not find a way to place his thoughts in a proper five paragraph package. And so it came to pass, alas, that young Tom succeeded at the competency test but failed to write. ❐

— *Cynthia Ellwood is principal at Hartford Avenue University School in Milwaukee.*

David Levine is an assistant professor of education at the University of North Carolina-Chapel Hill.

This article first appeared in Rethinking Schools, Vol. 1, #2, Spring 1987.

Changing Ethics

In North Carolina, teaching to the test was once considered unethical. Now it is all but blatantly encouraged.

BY PETER SACKS

In the accountability-obsessed 1990s, testing and teaching practices condemned as unethical and educationally unsound a decade earlier became de rigueur in North Carolina.

In 1988, the state of North Carolina enacted a Testing Code of Ethics that laid out proper testing procedures for teachers and schools, having adopted national models for testing ethics that were used in many states at the time. Among the most striking features of the document was its vigorous caveat against any attempts by teachers or schools to extensively coach and drill schoolchildren for upcoming standardized exams, known in the parlance of educators as "teaching the test."

Coming in the wake of a surge in testing in the 1980s, the North Carolina ethics code was undoubtedly founded on a heightened awareness among educators of the growing evidence documenting many unwholesome effects of teaching to tests. Indeed, the 1988 ethics code provided little room for interpretation, warning that:

> Coaching of students on specific test content or dissemination of test materials (including reproductions or modifications) prior to testing is not permitted. Such procedures will make results invalid. However, it is desirable to teach students general test-taking skills in order to make them aware of strategies that could enhance their performance on tests.

Elsewhere in the same document, the code writers also cautioned testers on the proper uses of tests, pointing out that test scores are but one of many indicators of performance. Again, the code's authors were quite explicit, writing that *"test scores should never be used in formal teacher or principal evaluations"* (emphasis added).

The 1988 ethics code didn't stop there. In several instances throughout the document, we find such cautions repeated as many as two or three times:

- "Instructional content should not be geared solely to preparing students to score well on standardized tests."

- "Although students should be told the general content of any upcoming standardized test and taught good test-taking skills, they are not to be drilled or coached on specific test content."

- "Scores on standardized tests must not be the sole determinant of whether a student is to be retained or promoted."

- "The curriculum is not to be taught simply to raise test scores. The weaknesses of students as revealed by test scores are expected to be considered in curriculum planning."

By the late 1990s, however, North Carolina's testing code of ethics had been changed dramatically with educators' and politicians' unabated obsession with educational crimes and punishments. Teaching and testing practices once condemned as not only unethical but as educational malpractice became routine in many states and school districts, including North Carolina. Nowadays, test-driven educators can blithely justify teaching to tests as simply teaching the state's designated curriculum for math, reading, or science.

Accordingly, the North Carolina 1996 revision to its testing code of ethics contained no mention whatsoever of any ill effects of teaching to tests. In fact, the new ethics code even appeared to encourage the practice, advising that testing should include "teaching the tested curriculum and test-preparation skills."

Test preparation skills, of course, is highly ambiguous, but it clearly permits practices that go well beyond general test taking skills. Hence, under the revised North Carolina code of ethics, all manner of test coaching and drilling — short of outright cheating — became not only acceptable, but were strongly encouraged. ❐

> **Testing practices once condemned as unethical became routine in many states.**

— Reprinted from Standardized Minds: The High Price of America's Testing Culture and What We Can Do to Change It *(New York: Perseus, 1999).*

FAILING OUR KIDS:
WHY THE TESTING CRAZE WON'T FIX OUR SCHOOLS

Jean-Claude Lejeune

Standards, Testing, And Race

Standards: Decoy Or Quality Control?

It is a travesty to expect all children to reach the same standards when only a few receive adequate resources.

BY
ASA HILLIARD

Is the standards movement a quality control movement, as it is advertised, or is it a decoy for something else?

We have been here before, with the standards movement. In fact, we reach a standards movement almost every three or four years. Some governor wants to manipulate the test score requirements or get a new test. Some president wants to manipulate test score requirements or get a new test. Somebody wants to change the standards of education, presumably as a way of raising the quality of schools and schooling and the achievement of children. I say presumably because I don't think that I can remember a time when that was really the reason for having a standards movement. If you want to raise quality, then standards manipulation is probably the last place that you would start.

Let me say at the outset that no one fears high standards, at least no Africans that I know. We do not fear clear standards. We do not fear uniform standards. We do not fear public standards. In fact, we have been at the forefront of standards of the highest order. [Asa Hilliard, Barbara Sizemore, et al, Saving the African American Child. Washington, DC: National Alliance of Black School Educators, 1984.]

But what we need is honest school improvement that acknowledges both high standards and high quality of school input. The standards movement as it is now progressing at the national and state level is half the solution to the problem. To establish the standards of output without having standards of input is a travesty. To hold children responsible for outcomes without giving the same level of sophisticated attention to guaranteeing the standards of exposure is an abandonment of the responsibility of adults for the education and socialization of children.

That's why I used the title that I did: "Standards as Quality Control or Decoy?" I believe that the standards movement is generally a decoy. I don't care whether it's a Democrat or a Republican who calls for it. Usually, when people put so much emphasis on standards as a school reform tool, it means that they want to look like they're performing a reform effort, but they're actually moonwalking. They look like they're going forward but they're going backwards.

What most of us fear is that we will be held responsible for achievement without being given the same quality of treatment on the front end. We're not afraid of standards. We're afraid of hurdles, of obstacles.

Assessment and Instruction

There are several things to deconstruct here, because they're all tied together. When we say standards, you can talk about setting standards. You can also talk about the instruments to measure the standards, whether they're valid, invalid, biased, or unbiased. And you can talk about the quality of instruction to enable people to meet the standards. All of that is tied together. But we generally break these apart. As a result, we usually make mistakes in our analysis. If you're talking

about using standards to get the achievement level of Americans up to snuff, then you're going to have to talk more broadly and deeply than we've been talking so far.

I'm a little bit tired of people getting credit for improving education by doing the cheapest thing they can do, which is to call for the manipulation of test scores or to create new standards. These new standards are not going to be any better than the ones the College Board developed in the College Board's Green Book: *What Students Need to Know and Do in Order to Graduate from College*. They're not going to be any higher or better than the standards of the National Alliance of Black School Educators. [Hilliard and Sizemore, et al, *Saving the African-American Child*. Washington, DC: National Alliance of Black School Educators, 1984]. In fact, I'll take any standards that you come up with as long as they're high enough. If you get a consensus of a group of thinking people, I don't think you can write a set of standards that won't make sense.

Are you going to say "no" to calculus as a standard for the high school level? I think calculus is a reasonable standard. All children are brilliant enough to learn calculus, if you want to offer it to them. But if you want to teach calculus, you have to know calculus. And most teachers don't. So

why blame the child for the inability to achieve when the deficiency is in the other place? Obviously, if you want the child to achieve in calculus and teachers don't know calculus, then now you've got to prepare the teachers. Now you're talking about staff development. See how it's all connected?

If someone really wants to raise the achievement of children, you've got to recognize reality in the classroom. Once you do so, you'll know that we'll have to do what we did in the 1960s. When this country thought that the Russians were ahead in the space race, when they put up Sputnik, the next thing that happened was that the U.S. massively mobilized for science education. It was science, science everywhere. We had a National Defense Education Act. Look at the language: education became a matter of national defense. When the rubber met the road, they knew they had to do something and they funded the process of doing it.

What's happening now? The budget is bankrupt on social welfare issues and nobody wants to do anything about it. So you manipulate the standards to make it look as if you're doing something. But you cannot fix the problems that are wrong in the public sector without providing resources.

If you want to reform schools, don't do it with testing. We used to say, "If you want elephants to grow, you don't weigh the elephants. You feed the elephants." Children will not grow unless they get quality instruction.

In some ways, I see the standards movement as Trivial Pursuit. We know it's not a reform tool and yet we move ahead as if it's a reform tool. I know why we ended up with national standards. After the Republicans gutted the social services budget, the politicians still wanted to look good to the people, so they could say they were making the best effort they could under the circumstances. In other words, they had to address the question, "What can I do with no money?" Basically, nothing but showboat.

IQ Is a Scam

I also want to say something about irrationality and mental measurement, because part of this job is to find tests that tell us the truth. The mental measurement movement is typified by irrationality.

IQ is the biggest scam in the history of education. Nobody needs IQ testing. Nobody benefits when you do it. I'm in a very different position than most of you; I don't want an IQ test for Black kids, and one for green kids, and one for yellow kids, and one for red kids. I don't want any for anybody, because it offers no benefits to anyone. The issue is not bias. Sometimes, people get up here to discuss bias, when we should be asking, "Why is this foolish question about IQ being asked? Who said that a teacher has to know a child's ultimate capability before they start to teach?"

I have friends who are abandoning IQ because they know it's hot water right now, at least the old IQ test. Now they're all running to the Seven Intelligences measurement, so that we can have seven ways to rank kids instead of one. The problem is, the purpose of testing does not change when you shift from the one-dimensional intelligence to the seven-dimensional intelligence. If your purpose is to rank, rather than to diagnose and to fix, then you never shifted paradigms. You just changed the language. Maybe you changed some of the activity.

I was on a panel with Howard Gardner, author of *Multiple Intelligences*, and I asked him, "Do you know what people are doing with your tests? They say, 'Well, you don't have mathematical intelligence but maybe you have artistic intelligence, maybe a little musical intelligence.'" He said,

Administering IQ tests is a professional welfare program.

"Well, I didn't mean that by that." I said, "I know. I didn't think you did. I think your constructs have much more to do with curriculum than they do with 'intelligence.'"

We have got to learn to ask new questions and not simply give a Black version of the white question. So intelligence testing should go out the window, as far as I'm concerned. Now if you want to know how we know it's irrational, get the book edited by Helga Rowe, *Intelligence: Reconceptualization and Measurement*, which are papers from a summit meeting of psychologists in mental measurement in Melbourne, Australia, in 1988. They were trying to figure out what was the state of the art in measurement, especially intelligence measurement, and they came away with three conclusions. Actually, there were probably more conclusions, but these are the three that interested me:

■ They couldn't agree on what intelligence was. That's what you might call a construct validity problem. It's a little hard to measure precisely when you don't have agreement on the construct.

■ There's no predictive validity to IQ tests unless you use low-level thinking as your achievement criteria. If you use high-level, complex, conceptually-oriented problem solving, then there's no correlation between IQ scores and achievement outcomes. This is serious, because that's where the IQ test is supposed to be making its contribution, in predictive validity. But it's not there unless you measure something that somebody has already had time to process.

■ If they can ever agree on what intelligence is, and if they can ever measure it, they will have to take context into account. That's what the Black psychologists have been arguing for before I was born: that the context is what gives meaning to a response. You can't universalize a dialogue, linguistically or culturally. It's scientific idiocy to do so. So you have to understand whose IQ is being tested — those who make the irrational IQ tests. IQ testing doesn't do any good for anybody other than people who need work. It's a professional welfare program.

The disproportionate placement of African-American males in classes for the mentally retarded should have taught a prudent person that something is wrong with intelligence testing. When you get 25% of African-American males in Mississippi public schools in classes for the mentally retarded — and no other group has a proportion like that — maybe there's something with the tests that we ought to look at. But if you're irrational, you don't. You go ahead as if it couldn't be your test.

IQ tests, universally, are invalid. You cannot measure in absence of understanding of the context of the person. That means their culture, that means the political situation, that means their exposure to curriculum — all of that adds up to context.

Standards and Curriculum

I'm often called on to testify in court cases. In one case in Florida, the judge asked me, very impatiently, "Well, just give me an example of a biased item!" I said, "Well, Judge, all of them are biased." And he said, "No, no, no. I don't want to hear that; I want to hear a specific example!" I said, "Well, OK."

The transgressions are so gross in these tests, it's so easy. That's a softball question for me. So I said, "You know, let's take this section here of this test. This is about geography, the section on geography." He said, "Well, what's wrong with it?" I said, "Florida doesn't teach geography."

Wouldn't you think that would be a content validity problem? He reluctantly had to rule in favor of the plaintiffs. Afterwards, officials actually had to go back and institute a statewide curricu-

lum in Florida. So now Florida has a curriculum, supposedly. They went through a process and now they say, "We have a curriculum, so we can have a test, and we can make measurement." But all they really have is a standard measure with no match between the standard and what is actually taught in school.

We're going to run the risk of the same thing at the national level. Why? I sat on a subcommittee of the Goals 2000 national goals panel when they were talking about national standards. One of the biggest problems they had was political, because the states don't want to be dictated to. Each state will set its own standards, if it wants to set standards. This potentially means 50 standards. But you're going to have one test, at the national level, to measure the 50 different standards? That's irrational. That means you can't be serious about what you said you were wanting to do.

I could go on. But the issue is, when we finally get down to the end of this standard dialogue, where will we stand on national assessment? What kind of assessment, achievement or otherwise? Will the assessment be rational? Will it be true content validity? Will there be an empirical way to test it or will we still fool ourselves on mental measurement?

There's also the question of a common national curriculum. If you're not ready for a national curriculum, you're not going to have national stan-

Joel Pett, Lexington Herald Leader

dards. And you certainly won't have national, standardized assessment, because there'll be a mismatch between the assessment and the sets of standards that go with each state, and maybe even substandards within each state.

Opportunity to Learn

The real issue is one of common treatment, that is, opportunity to learn. One of the things we find is that there are a lot of people that don't want all children to learn at the highest level. I read Lisa Delpit's book, *Other People's Children*, and it's clear there are a lot of people that don't want to teach other people's children, that don't want to pay for other people's children's education.

Let me give you the bottom line on vouchers. The voucher movement is a movement of greedy people who don't want to pay for other people's children. They're trying to get money into their pockets so they can pay for the private schools they're already paying for. They give my child $1,800 in a voucher, let him show up at the Moon Glow Private School that's charging $12,000 a year tuition with his $1,800 voucher, and say, "I would come to school over here, but I don't have transportation either, and all I got is this voucher." Do you think that's a solution to the educational needs of the masses of our children, black or white? It isn't.

It's disingenuous of those people who support vouchers to say what they're trying to do is school reform. What they're trying to do is get their greedy paws on another couple bucks to reduce their private school tuition. That's what it's about. I told you I was going to tell it to you exactly the way it is.

What I want to talk about is the common treatment opportunity, that is, opportunity to learn. You can't hold children to the standards unless you give them a chance to master those standards. You have to check to see if the opportunities are there. We are a country typified by savage inequalities — I love the title of Jonathan Kozol's work, *Savage Inequalities* — and it's not the children who are savages, it's the people who savagely distribute the resources inequitably. Here's what Kozol finds out: $10,000 per year per child at New Trier Township High School. $5,000 per year per child at DuSable High School. Where you live determines what level of resources you get. That's a policy issue that is not being addressed by the standards movement. They're not even looking at the inequality. They're looking only at the output, not the input.

Content validity of achievement tests, and the standards, and the curriculum — all three must be

Jean-Claude Lejeune

aligned with each other. But I see no hope that that's going to happen in this country any time soon. Too many vested interests have reason not to see that happen.

Quality Teaching

Another problem is that many of the people who are talking standards have no idea of the importance of quality teaching and leadership. I was senior advisor on a video series with Dr. Barbara Sizemore [*Every Child Can Succeed*, Agency for Instructional Technology, Bloomington, IN] looking mainly at public schools where the children from the lowest quartile in economics are performing in the top quartile and higher in academics. How often do you think that happens? Well, I can tell you it happens a lot. We started with some of the schools that Barbara had been working with in the Hill District in Pittsburgh. The kids are all coming out of the housing projects, through the crack-infested neighborhoods, through the gang-banging neighborhoods. The Vann school and Madison school in that neighborhood are number one and number two. They have good leadership and good teaching, which accounts for their quality output. Unless we accept that good teaching is efficacious, that it can move kids in a profound way, then all the discussion about standards will have no meaning whatsoever.

We also need to locate and destroy what I call "doubt production." As an academic, I'm interested in origin of doubt, especially the doubt that all children can learn. I got a chance to speak at the American Psychological Association last August on the racism in psychology. One of the things that I charged was that the association itself contained members who for years have been manufacturers of doubt. The ideology of the absence of intelligence of African people was constructed by several of the most prestigious psychologists that we know.

What to Do?

If you want to do something, instead of manipulating the standards, go into the programs that teach the genetic inferiority of people of color, in psychology programs, in sociology programs. Go into those places and undo what is being done. For example, there's a book by Mark Snyderman and Stanley Rothman, *The IQ Controversy*, 1990. In the book, over 1,000 prestigious psychologists were surveyed and over half of them agreed with the conclusion of *The Bell Curve* with respect to the difference between Black and White IQ. In other words, they believe that the IQ test is valid, which means that the gap in intelligence is real and it's not just a gap in test scores. Now when the elite of the profession still profess this publicly, you've got a problem of the manufacture of doubt. How are you going to fix the school if on the one end people are talking about how all children can learn, and on the other end they're talking about how Black children aren't as intelligent as white kids?

So where do we go from here? As I said, we need to connect standards with instruction so that the standards themselves are content-valid, and then we need to connect the assessment instrument to the standards. If that happens, then maybe we can make some moves forward.

I have no expectation that that's going to happen, however. Therefore, I think the standards movement is going to be abandoned and we'll be doing this again in another five years when somebody else has the problem of how to raise achievement with no money.

But if we can turn the discussion around so that it focuses on the quality of service rather than on the analysis of children and their families, then maybe, just maybe, we might be one step ahead when the topic comes up again. ❑

—The above is condensed from a speech by Asa Hilliard, professor of urban education at Georgia State University in Atlanta. Hilliard is the author of numerous books and articles on education, particularly the education of African-American children, and his most recent book is SBA: The Reawakening of the African Mind (Gainseville, FL: Makare Publishers).

The article was published in Rethinking Schools, Vol. 12, #4, Summer 1998.

The Bell Curve: Stealth Book of the 1990's

For anyone who thinks that *The Bell Curve*, did not have an impact on public policy, guess again.

"The biggest-selling race book of the decade was *The Bell Curve*, which not only polarized the perception of race in America but had a tremendous influence over public policy," according to ABC news correspondent Farai Chideya in her book *The Color of Our Future*, (New York: William Morrow & Co., 1999, p. 23).

Bell Curve co-author Charles Murray has made similar statements. In a 1997 interview in *The National Review*, Murray was asked why his book was not cited more in national debates around issues such as affirmative action and welfare reform.

Murray's response noted in part that "A lot of silence about *The Bell Curve* can be put down to political cowardice."

"Affirmative action was still politically sacrosanct when *The Bell Curve* came out in October 1994," Murray said. "Within a year, the tide had swung decisively. Did the book play any role? Damned if I know. ..."

"My best guess — and the broad answer to your question — is that *The Bell Curve* is the stealth public-policy book of the 1990s. It has created a subtext on a range of issues. Everybody knows what the subtext is. Nobody says it out loud." ❑

— Barbara Miner

Pencils Out!

Here's a chance to see what's on the 10th grade history and social sciences test in Massachusetts.

BY DERRICK Z. JACKSON

Get out your No. 2 pencils. Judge for yourself whether the MCAS 10th grade history and social sciences test is the kind of test students need for tomorrow's jobs.

The following are several of what the Massachusetts Department of Education calls its "common" questions. In the 12 different forms of the test, these are the items that every student must answer.

■ King Henry issued the Edict of Nantes in 1598 to (a) end the Hundred Years' War in England; (b) establish Quebec as a French colony; (c) grant religious tolerance to French Protestants (Huguenots); (d) give the Estates General power to control taxes.

■ The prosperity of the African kingdom of Ghana was based upon its (a) domination of the gold trade; (b) easy access to sea routes to Arabia; (c) powerful military forces; (d) advanced system of roads and canals.

■ Which phrase best describes the feudal system in medieval Europe? (a) the concentration of all political power in the central government; (b) the competition between medieval nation-states for supremacy; (c) the collective ownership of land; (d) the exchange of service for land.

■ The Line of Demarcation drawn through South America by the Treaty of Tordesillas (1494) was an attempt by Pope Alexander VI to (a) control the slave trade; (b) prevent Portugal and Spain from fighting over colonies; (c) establish a new trade route to the West Indies; (d) slow down the growth of colonial business and industry.

■ King Henry VIII (1509-1547) is known for leading England's (a) discovery of the New World; (b) conquest of Poland; (c) division of Parliament into the Houses of Lords and Commons; (d) separation from the Roman Catholic Church.

■ When European exploration of the Americas began, most European governments were (a) monarchies; (b) democracies; (c) theocracies; (d) anarchies.

■ Which of the following will most likely decrease the demand for labor? (a) a decrease in the supply of available workers; (b) an increase in goods and services produced by workers; (c) a decrease in demand for goods and services; (d) an increase in the training and education level of workers.

Why did King Henry issue the Edict of Nantes in 1598? What happens when interest rates decline?

■ Which of the following will probably occur when interest rates decline? (a) food production will decrease; (b) consumer borrowing will increase; (c) home purchases will decrease; (d) mortgage rates will increase.

■ An anonymous poet in medieval times described the three social estates (classes) of European society in the following way: One toils the fields, one prays, and one defends. (a) name the three medieval social estates. (b) describe the characteristics of each estate.

■ Throughout human history, humans have transported plants or animals from one region of the world to another. Listed below are some of those plants and animals. Read and think about the list to answer parts a, b, and c: potato, tobacco, horse, corn, wheat; (a) Write the name of one of the plants or animal listed above and state where it was originally found; (b) Who transported the plant or animal you selected, and where did they take it? (c) Explain the effects of the plant or animal on the lives of the people who received it.

■ Voltaire and Rousseau were writers during the (a) Industrial Revolution; (b) Reformation; (c) Middle Ages; (d) Enlightenment.

■ World War I began almost immediately after (a) ratification of the Treaty of Versailles; (b) outbreak of the Boxer Rebellion; (c) assassination of Archduke Francis Ferdinand; (d) seizure of Bosnia by the Ottoman Empire.

■ Most European rivalries for imperial territory in the late 1800s occurred in (a) Australia; (b) South America; (c) North America; (d) Africa.

■ Hereditary succession is a practice most often associated with (a) communism; (b) monarchy; (c) democracy; (d) fascism.

■ A capitalist economy typically includes all of the following except (a) state-owned factories; (b) private property; (c) profit motive; (d) market competition.

■ In 1928 the first of a series of Five Year Plans for rapid industrialization was developed by the central government of (a) Soviet Union; (b) Nigeria. (c) United States; (d) Japan.

■ In the 1930s and 1940s, the need for which natural resource contributed most to Japan's military expansion into Southeast Asia? (a) copper; (b) uranium; (c) oil; (d) gold.

■ Which paired group listed below advocated "passive resistance" and "civil disobedience?" (a) Viet Cong and Viet Minh; (b) IRA and PLO; (c) Red Guard and Bolsheviks; (d) independence movement in India and the civil rights movement in America.

■ The post-World War II United States foreign policy of containment was meant to (a) limit the spread of communism; (b) hold down worldwide inflation; (c) limit illegal immigration; (d) halt the spread of nuclear weapons.

■ In 1949 the Chinese Nationalist government that fled to Taiwan was led by (a) Mao Zedong; (b) Ho Chi Minh; (c) Ngo Dinh Diem; (d) Chiang Kai-shek.

■ The Soviet equivalent of the North Atlantic Treaty Organization was the (a) Popular Front; (b) Comintern; (c) Warsaw Pact; (d) Kuomintang.

Answers (compiled by Globe Staff):

1 (c) 2 (a) 3 (d) 4 (b) 5 (d) 6 (a) 7 (c) 8 (b) 9 (essay) 10 (essay) 11 (d) 12 (c) 13 (d) 14 (b) 15 (a) 16 (a) 17 (c) 18 (d) 19 (a) 20 (d) 21 (c).

— *Derrick Z. Jackson is a columnist for the Boston Globe.*

The above is reprinted from his column of June 9, 2000. Reprinted with permission.

Jean-Claude Lejeune

Our Nation's Past

*Here are questions about pivotal events in American history —
although they are unlikely to appear on an official standardized test.*

BY DERRICK Z. JACKSON

For my annual alternative to the Fourth of July column, get out your No. 2 pencils again. Recently I published questions from the MCAS 10th-grade history test, criticizing them as being grossly Eurocentric and of questionable relevance for today's job seekers.

Of course, many readers saw nothing wrong with the questions. One wrote that surgeons, construction workers, and software designers may not need to know about the Edict of Nantes or the Treaty of Tordesillas at work but that such events "are not trivia - they are part of the framework within which we try to evaluate our own nation's attempts to shape the world."

Let us be nice and assume the reader is correct. But if you are going to be correct about how our own nation shaped itself, you have to have other questions that are not on the MCAS tests:

■ According to Goree Island's slave museum, the number of stolen Africans is the equivalent of emptying out the current metropolitan areas of:

(a) Milwaukee; (b) Tokyo; (c) Los Angeles; (d) New York, Los Angeles, Chicago, Washington, San Francisco, and Philadelphia combined.

■ According to most histories, the number of stolen Africans who actually made it alive to the Americas is the equivalent of:

(a) New York, Los Angeles, Chicago, Washington, San Francisco, and Philadelphia combined; (b) New York, Los Angeles, and Chicago combined; (c) Los Angeles and Chicago combined; (d) just San Francisco and Philadelphia.

■ The conservative value of slave labor to the

> *The conservative value of slave labor to the American economy, when it was analyzed in 1983, is nearly the equivalent of the 1999 spending budget for:*
>
> *(a) Wisconsin; (b) The Rolling Stones Tour; (c) The New York Yankees; (d) The United States.*

American economy, when it was analyzed in 1983, is nearly the equivalent of the 1999 spending budget for:

(a) Wisconsin; (b) The Rolling Stones Tour; (c) The New York Yankees; (d) The United States.

■ The high estimate of the value of slave labor to the American economy is $2 \frac{1}{2}$ times that of the 1999 budget for:

(a) France; (b) Japan; (c) The New York Yankees; (d) The United States.

■ The World War II generation will bequeath $8 trillion to its children. In the years 1929 to 1969, wages lost by African-Americans to discrimination were:

(a) nothing, because we are now a color-blind society; (b) $1.6 billion; (c) irrelevant because Michael Jordan owns part of the Washington Wizards and Magic Johnson owns part of the Los Angeles Lakers; (d) $1.6 trillion, nearly equal to 1999 federal budget of $1.7 trillion.

■ One result of post-slavery discrimination is that the average white baby boomer and the average black baby boomer will respectively inherit:

(a) $50,000 and $42,000; (b) $80,000 and $50,000; (c) $20,000 and $15,000; (d) $65,000 and $8,000.

■ The term "40 Acres and a Mule" traces its roots to:

(a) Spike Lee movies; (b) an overly optimistic Mississippi racetrack owner; (c) Thomas Jefferson's heartfelt wish to free the slaves; (d) General Sherman's Field Order 15.

■ Under "40 Acres and a Mule," about 40,000 newly freed slaves were given Southern coastal land that had been abandoned by unpardoned Confederate families. These black people held the land for two years before angry white people stole it through beatings, torture, and legal chicanery. During those two years, the black occupants were known for:

(a) being lazy and shiftless; (b) being top local athletes; (c) wanting back the good old days, where you could depend on a bowl of gruel and a watermelon from massa; (d) fine crops and self-governance.

■ New England is far from cotton fields and sugar plantations. Thus it is interesting that Brown University:

(a) created a chair in honor of abolitionist John Brown; (b) named its music department after James Brown; (c) named its graduate school of business after Ron Brown; (d) was founded by the Browns of Rhode Island, who profited from the triangular slave trade.

■ The largest taxpayer in the colony of Rhode Island in 1775 made his money through:

(a) whaling; (b) online trading; (c) cranberries; (d) slave trading.

■ New England's exports to the West Indies in 1772 amounted to:

(a) very little because New Englanders were appalled by slave sugar plantations; (b) very little because Federal Express did not exist yet; (c) very little because of an explosion of free trade with England; (d) two-thirds of New England's exports.

■ In Lowell, Mass., in 1835, politicians, law enforcement, lawyers, doctors, and shopkeepers signed petitions to:

(a) call for the end of slavery; (b) volunteer to go south for a Freedom Summer to understand the plight of the slaves; (c) build a new Fenway Park for the Red Sox; (d) oppose abolition because the textile mills depended on slave-picked cotton.

■ African-Americans fought in every US war, hoping their participation would result in equality. After the Civil War, World War I, and World War II, black sacrifice for America and the world was rewarded with:

(a) full voting rights; (b) free tickets to Jack Johnson and Joe Louis fights; (c) free coupons for watermelon; (d) lynchings and white race riots.

By the way, the answer is (d) on all questions. ❐

— Derrick Z. Jackson is a columnist for the Boston Globe, where this appeared on July 4, 2000. Reprinted with permissison.

AP / Wide World Photos

The Little Rock Nine desegregated Little Rock High School, but only with the protection of federal troops.

Testing's Unequal Impact

The high-stakes testing craze hurts poor students and students of color the most.

BY GARY ORFIELD AND JOHANNA WALD

Despite the political popularity of the testing "solution," many educators and civil rights advocates are suggesting that it has actually exacerbated the problems it sought to alleviate. They claim that these [high-stakes testing] policies discriminate against minority students, undermine teachers, reduce opportunities for students to engage in creative and complex learning assignments, and deny high school diplomas because of students' failure to pass subjects they were never taught. They argue that using tests to raise academic standards makes as much sense as relying upon thermometers to reduce fevers. Most compellingly, they maintain that these tests are directing sanctions against the victims, rather than the perpetrators, of educational inequities.

The implications of these arguments were serious enough to lead The Civil Rights Project at Harvard University to commission a series of studies on the educational and social impact of high-stakes testing policies from some of the nation's top scholars in this field. Some of their most significant findings include:

■ High-stakes tests attached to grade promotion and high school graduation lead to increased dropout rates, particularly for minority students. George Madaus and Marguerite Clarke of Boston College discovered a strong association between high-stakes testing and increased dropout rates. They cite studies showing that in 1986, half of the ten states with the lowest dropout figures used no high-stakes tests. The other half employed testing programs that could be characterized as low stakes. Nine of the ten states with the highest dropout rates used standardized tests in decisions about high school graduation.

> *High-stakes tests can lead to increased dropout rates, particularly for students of color.*

The effects for minority students can be discerned from a study by Aaron Pallas of Michigan State University and Gary Natriello of Columbia University, who examined the racial and ethnic disparities in performance on the Texas Assessment of Academic Skills (TAAS) between 1996 and 1998. By the spring of their senior year, almost twice as many Black and Hispanic students as White students had not passed the TAAS exit-level tests required to obtain a Texas high school diploma. The authors concluded that "these tests are, and will remain for some time, an impediment to the graduation prospects of African-American and Hispanic youth." In another study, Columbia's Jay Heubert points out that students of color are almost always overrepresented among those who are denied diplomas on the basis of test scores.

No Lasting Benefits

■ Using tests to retain students in the same grade produces no lasting educational benefits. Robert Hauser of the University of Wisconsin has found that retaining students in the same grade creates huge management problems in the classroom, is extremely expensive for the school system, and dramatically increases the likelihood that the retained student will eventually drop out. Moreover, African-American males are disproportionately represented among those who are held back. The congressionally mandated 1999 National Academy of Sciences report "High Stakes: Testing for Tracking, Promotion and Graduation" cites five other studies that draw similar conclusions about the negative effects of retaining students.

If, as all these studies suggest, high-stakes tests both discriminate against poor and minority students and are educationally unsound, we are still left with the dilemma of how to achieve the dual goals of equity and excellence. Dozens of studies offer convincing evidence that children in poor schools make academic gains when they have access to quality early-childhood education programs, when they are taught in small classes by skilled and committed teachers, and when they are given assessments linked to appropriate and immediate responses.

Competent Teachers

The single most important factor in raising academic performance in poor schools appears to be the presence of experienced, competent, and caring teachers. Disadvantaged youths currently are taught by the least prepared and most transient instructors in the system. Devising incentives for recruiting and maintaining highly qualified teachers and for retraining existing staff in high-poverty schools should be the top priority of those serious about raising standards. ❑

— The above is excerpted from the article "Testing, Testing," in the June 5, 2000 issue of The Nation. Reprinted with permission.

Skjold Photographs

ORGANIZATIONAL POSITION

National Council of La Raza

The following is excerpted from a statement released April 4, 2000 by Raul Yza-guirre, president of the National Council of La Raza, a nationwide advocacy group.

"Latinos are an increasing segment of the current school population and the future workforce, and obtaining better educational outcomes for Latino students is vital for our nation's prosperity. Unfortunately, these children are seldom challenged to meet high academic standards and are often denied the opportunity to take rigorous classwork. High-quality tests can be a good tool for improving schooling and holding school systems accountable for helping all children meet high standards. However, they should never be the only measure used for making high-stakes decisions that will have a dramatic impact on these children's lives."

The Forgotten History of Eugenics

'High-stakes' testing has its origins in the eugenics movement and racist assumptions about IQ. We forget, at our own peril, that this legacy hangs over current demands for increased testing.

BY ALAN STOSKOPF

At the beginning of the century, one of the most damaging experiments in public education began. Under the banner of educational reform, the American eugenics movement captured the hearts and minds of some of the nation's most influential educational researchers and policy makers. While the history of the eugenics movement has been virtually written out of American history textbooks, it nonetheless has had an insidious effect on the lives of students and the organization of public schools. It also has become part of an unexamined legacy that shadows today's standards and testing movement.

What was eugenics? The English mathematician Sir Francis Galton first coined the term in 1883. He wrote, "Eugenics is the study of the agencies under social control that seek to improve or impair the racial qualities of future generations either physically or mentally."[1] What Galton saw as a new branch of scientific inquiry became a dogmatic prescription in the ranking and ordering of human worth. His ideas found their most receptive audience at the turn of the century in the United States.

Eugenics fed off of the fears of white middle and upper class Americans. In the early 20th century, the United States was experiencing rapid social and economic change. As the nation became more industrial and urban, millions of poor immigrants from southern and eastern Europe flocked to the United States seeking a better life. Simultaneously, thousands of African-Americans were beginning a great migration to northern cities from the Jim Crow South. Competition for jobs intensified existing frictions along class and racial lines.

Periodic economic recessions created further social unrest. Labor unions, civil rights groups, and the woman's suffrage movement pressed for greater equity. At the same time nativist and racist groups like the Ku Klux Klan pulled in the opposite direction. It was out of this cauldron of social upheaval that the American eugenics movement emerged. It promised prosperity and progress, not through strikes or ugly race riots, but through a new science that would combine advances in the field of genetics with the efficiency of the assembly line.

Crude Interpretations

Eugenicists used a flawed and crude interpretation of Gregor Mendel's laws on heredity to argue that criminality, intelligence, and pauperism were passed down in families as simple dominant or recessive hereditary traits. Mainline eugenicists (those eugenicists who were explicitly preoccupied with issues of race), believed that some individuals and entire groups of people (such as Southern Europeans, Jews, Africans, and Latinos) were more predisposed to the "defective genes." Charles Davenport, a leader in American eugenics, argued for laws to control the spread of "inferior blood" into the general population. He told an international gathering of scholars "that the biological basis for such laws is doubtless an appreciation of the fact that negroes and other races carry traits that do not go well with our social organization."[2]

Davenport's wishes were partly realized. Eugenic advocates convinced 30 state legislatures to pass involuntary sterilization laws that targeted "defective strains" within the general population, such as the blind, deaf, epileptic, feebleminded, and paupers. On the national level, eugenic supporters played a decisive role in the Congressional passage of the draconian Immigration and Restriction Act of 1924, which established blatantly racist quotas. President Calvin Coolidge embraced the eugenic assumptions behind the law when he declared, "America must be kept American. Bio-

A display from the American Eugenics Society at a fair in Topeka, KS, in 1929. The sign on the top, for example, reads: "Every 15 seconds, $100 of your money goes for the care of persons with bad heredity, such as the insane, feeble-minded, criminals, and other defectives."

logical laws show … that Nordics deteriorate when mixed with other races."[3]

While those laws have been repealed, the impact of eugenics on public education was more enduring. Eugenic ideology worked its way into the educational reform movements of the 1910s and 20s, playing a key role in teacher training, curriculum development, and school organization. It also provided the guiding ideology behind the first IQ tests. Those tests were used to track students into separate and unequal education courses, establish the first gifted and talented programs, and promote the idea that educational standards could be measured through single-numbered scores. Eugenic ideas about the intellectual worth of students penetrated deeply into the fabric of American education.

Eugenics was a common feature in college curricula. Universities "offering courses in eugenics increased from 44 in 1914 to 376 in 1928."[4] A recent analysis of 41 high school biology textbooks used through the 1940s revealed that nearly 90% of them had sections on eugenics.[5] Major figures in education were attracted to eugenics and wrote books for teachers and the general public. Eugenics became a top-down model of "education reform" for these educators. A cadre of university experts trained in the latest testing methods and embracing eugenic principles believed they could make schooling a more efficient enterprise. Schools would be the place where students both learned basic eugenic principles and also were tracked into their future roles as dictated by their biological worth.

Influential Textbooks

A sampling of influential textbooks used in colleges of education gives us a better sense of some of the eugenic visions of educational reform. Lewis Terman, Professor of Education at Stanford University and originator of the Stanford-Binet intelligence test, is remembered today as an early proponent of tracking. Not as well known is that his views on tracking and school organization were rooted in a eugenic conception of humanity.

Terman expressed these views in his textbook, *The Measurement of Intelligence* (1916). The book would be used for decades in teacher training. He wrote that:

> Among laboring men and servant girls there are thousands like them [feebleminded individuals]. They are the world's "hewers of wood and drawers of water." And yet, as far as intelligence is concerned, the tests have told the truth. No amount of school instruction will ever make them intelligent voters or capable voters in the true sense of the word.
>
> … The fact that one meets this type with such frequency among Indians, Mexicans, and Negroes suggests quite forcibly that the

whole question of racial differences in mental traits will have to be taken up anew and by experimental methods.

Children of this group should be segregated in special classes and be given instruction which is concrete and practical. They cannot master, but they can often be made efficient workers, able to look out for themselves. There is no possibility at present of convincing society that they should not be allowed to reproduce, although from a eugenic point of view they constitute a grave problem because of their unusually prolific breeding. (pp. 91-92)

Terman and other educational psychologists successively convinced many school districts to use high-stakes and culturally-biased tests to place "slow" students into special classes, rigid academic tracks, or entirely separate schools. The racist and class assumptions behind these recommendations were justified as scientifically sound because the "tests told the truth." IQ tests soon became the favorite eugenic tool for identifying "superior and inferior" students and then charting their educational destiny.

The tests were also seen as an instrument to identify students deserving special treatment. Today's gifted and talented programs had their origins in the eugenic use of IQ tests in the 1920s. Leta Hollingworth, a professor at Teachers College at Columbia University, was a founder and persuasive advocate of gifted and talented programs in schools. She and other educational leaders thought only the students from the right biological stock were capable of achieving high academic standards.

In *Gifted Children: Their Nature and Nurture* (1926), a book that is frequently cited by researchers of "gifted" programs today, [6] Hollingworth wrote:

One result recurs persistently wherever American children are tested by nationality of ancestors. American children of Italian parentage show a low average of intelligence. The selection of Italians received into this country has yielded very few gifted children. (p. 71)

[Eugenics would] ultimately reduce misery if the stupid, the criminal, and other mentally, physically, and morally deficient would refrain from reproduction. (p. 199) [7]

As with Terman, Hollingworth's ideas were not on the margins of educational thought. Eugenic themes proliferated in educational journals and textbooks from the 1910s through the 1930s. In particular, the popular belief took hold that IQ tests could label and accurately place students into academic tracks according to their inherited abilities. For example, an educational consultant for the San Jose school system recommended that the district use test scores to guide "children for their proper economic life activities in accordance with their abilities." The great majority of Mexican-American school children in the district were to assume lower academic tracks because the tests supposedly revealed their inferior intellectual quality. [8]

Testing on the Rise

We do not know all the ways eugenic notions affected public education. We do know that by the early 1920s, more than 2 million American school children were being tested primarily for academic tracking purposes.[9] At least some of the decisions to allocate resources and select students for academic or vocational courses were influenced by eugenic notions of student worth.

It is important to recognize that an active minority of educators, journalists, labor groups, and parents resisted these ideas. In particular, there were informed critiques by African-American scholars such as W. E. B. Du Bois, Horace Mann Bond, and Howard Long. They decried the use of these tests to rank racial groups. In "Intelligence Tests and Propaganda," Horace Mann Bond issued a warning about the misuse of IQ tests:

But so long as any group of men attempts to use these tests as funds of information for the approximation of crude and inaccurate generalizations, so long must we continue to cry "Hold!" To compare the crowded millions of New York's East Side with the children of Morningside Heights [an upper class neighborhood at the time] indeed involves a great contradiction; and to claim that the results of the tests given to such diverse groups, drawn from such varying strata of the social complex, are in any wise accurate, is to expose a fatuous sense of unfairness and lack of appreciation of the

> *Test scores are often seen as proxies for intelligence or important indicators of what students are learning.*

Jean-Claude Lejeune

great environmental factors of modern urban life. [10]

Too few white Americans read these words. It was not until the 1960s that these early rebuttals were widely recognized as important contributions to the body of academic literature refuting racist and biologically determinist interpretations of IQ tests.

Bond's cautions also were not heeded by Richard Herrnstein and Charles Murray when they wrote the best-selling *The Bell Curve* in 1994. Many reviewers within the academic and lay communities have criticized the thinly veiled racism and the voluminous but misleading use of data found in the book. These tendencies were reminiscent of the eugenic advocates' interpretation of tests in the 1920s. Furthermore, Murray and Herrnstein rewrote history when they claimed that the eugenic use of tests was not used to draw any negative conclusions about immigrant groups in the country and played no role in the immigration hearings of 1924.[11] It has been this kind of denial of history that makes it all the more important to re-examine how standardized tests are being used in educational reform today.

Standardized tests can provide important diagnostic information for educators. Achieving standards of academic excellence through ongoing assessment of student work is a vital component of a young person's learning. However, too often,

standards and assessment have become synonymous with top-down, externally mandated tests. Learning becomes reduced to test preparation and test taking. Test scores are often seen as proxies for intelligence or as the most important indicators of what students are learning. Quick judgments and quick fixes are the products of this kind of reform. And this phenomenon is not just a relic of the past.

Similar Consequences?

Even if many supporters of high-stakes tests might recoil at the assumptions underlying the use of standardized tests earlier in the century, the consequences of this version of education reform might not be so different from the 1920s. This becomes even more apparent when performances are compared between poorer and more affluent school districts. Doing well on these tests is strongly correlated with income levels and only reconfirms the educational inequities that have characterized American education throughout the century. The academic tracking begun by "yesterday's" eugenicists is an institutional legacy we live with today. Education reform that is driven by high-stakes tests stands a good chance of entrenching that legacy.

The history of eugenics in American education needs to be examined in more depth and brought to bear on arguments supporting the use of high stakes tests to raise academic standards in public schools. This history raises some challenging and disturbing questions for all of us today. What is the economic and political context in which the contemporary version of educational reform is being touted? What are the assumptions about student learning that fuel the current wave of testing? What are the effects of this testing on the lives of students and the educational climate of schools? How do these tests affect the equitable distribution of educational resources and opportunities between different school districts?

These questions need to be discussed with educational policy makers and representatives from diverse communities in open forums. Parents, students, and teachers have to be brought into these conversations. The eugenics movement is a reminder of what can happen when the assumptions and consequences of educational reform are not put to the test of real life experience. ❑

― *Alan Stoskopf (Alan_Stoskopf@Facing.org) is Associate Program Director for Professional Development at Facing History and Ourselves, a national non-profit educational foundation in Brookline, MA.. This article is based on research, done over the last eight years at Facing History and Ourselves, examining the history of the American eugenics movement.*

The above was published in Rethinking Schools, Vol. 13, #3, Spring, 1999.

FOR FURTHER READING:

Stephen Selden, Inheriting Shame: *The Story of Eugenics in America* (New York: Teachers College Press, 1999).

Russell Jacoby and Naomi Glauberman, ed. *The Bell Curve Debate: History, Documents, Opinions,* (New York: Times Books, Random House, 1995), chapters 6-8.

Alan Stoskopf, et al, *Confronting the Forgotten History of the American Eugenics Movement* (forthcoming from Harvard/Facing History Project, Fall 1999).

FOOTNOTES

[1] Francis Galton, *Inquiries into Human Faculty and its Development* (London: Macmillan, 1883), frontispiece.

[2] Steven Selden, "Conservative Ideology and Curriculum," *Educational Theory 3* (Summer, 1977), p. 218.

[3] Calvin Coolidge, "Whose Country is This?" *Good Housekeeping,* 72 (February, 1921), p. 14.

[4] Hamilton Cravens, *The Triumph of Evolution: American Scientists and the Heredity-Environment Controversy, 1900-1941* (Philadelphia: University of Pennsylvania Press, 1978), p. 53.

[5] Steven Selden, *Inheriting Shame: The Story of Eugenics in America* (New York: Teachers College Press, 1999), p. 64.

[6] Ibid, p. 102.

[7] Ibid, p. 103.

[8] David Tyack, *The One Best System: A History of American Urban Education* (Harvard University Press, 1974), p. 213.

[9] Sarah Glazer, "Intelligence Testing," *CQ Researcher* (July 30, 1993), p. 660.

[10] Horace Mann Bond, "Intelligence Tests and Propaganda," *The Crisis*, 28 (1924), p. 64.

[11] Richard Herrnstein and Charles Murray, *The Bell Curve: Intelligence and Class Structure in American Life* (New York: Free Press, 1994), p. 5.

QUOTABLE QUOTE

"Humans have evolved as a species to carry out at least seven kinds of computations or analyses: those involving language (linguistic intelligence, as exemplified by a poet); logical-mathematical analysis (in a scientist, mathematician, or logician); spatial representation (for instance, the painter, sculptor, architect, sailor, geometer, or engineer); musical analysis; bodily-kinesthetic thinking (for example, the dancer, athlete, mime, actor, surgeon, craftsman); and two forms of personal understanding — interpersonal knowledge (of other persons, as in a salesman, teacher, therapist, leader) and intrapersonal knowledge (the ability to know one's own desires, fears, and competences and to act productively on the basis of that knowledge.)

"According to my analysis, most formal testing — whatever the area that is allegedly being tested — engages primarily the linguistic and logical-mathematical faculties. If one has high linguistic and logical-mathematical intelligences, one is likely to do well in school and in formal testing. Poor endowment or learning in one or both of these intelligences is likely to result in poor standardized scores."

— *Howard Gardner, from his book Multiple Intelligences: The Theory in Practice.*

An Untold Story Of Resistance

African-American educators led the fight against IQ testing in the 1920s and '30s. Their struggle has important implications for today's fight against 'high-stakes' testing.

BY ALAN STOSKOPF

It was not until I was long out of school and indeed after the (first) World War that there came the hurried use of the new technique of psychological [IQ] tests, which were quickly adjusted so as to put black folk absolutely beyond the possibility of civilization. [1]

— W. E. B. Du Bois, 1940

The words of W. E. B. Du Bois still haunt us. We are now experiencing another onslaught and "hurried use" of tests in our schools. How African-American educators fought against their uses in the past has important implications for today's resistance to "high-stakes" testing.

We have grown accustomed to the constant refrain of schools needing to institute "world class standards" and be held accountable through externally based, high-stakes exams. Research and experience demonstrate that this version of "education reform" will negatively impact all students, especially students of color from lower income backgrounds. We also know that the best assessments originate in the classroom and are an ongoing part of a student's reflection of her or his progress. Few people realize that current critiques of testing and the calls for more authentic forms of assessment have been built in part upon the pioneering work of African-American intellectuals in the 1920s and 1930s.

An appreciation of what these educators did begins with race. The underside to the "Roaring '20s" was its violent racism and xenophobia. Jim Crow ruled. In the South an apartheid-like caste system enveloped daily life. In the North, African–Americans faced discrimination in housing, employment, the courts, and schools. The Ku Klux Klan reached its peak of popularity and claimed members in most states. Lynchings of African-American men were a familiar occurrence. Fears of racial impurity propelled the passage of the Immigration Restriction Act of 1924. (This act set draconian quotas based on race and nationality. It blatantly favored people of Northern and Western European ancestry and was not substantively revised until 1965.)

Even the liberal New Deal Era of the 1930s did not fundamentally alter striking social inequalities wrought by racism. As an economic depression engulfed the entire nation, the Roosevelt Administration initiated a variety of public works projects aimed at providing relief to ordinary Americans and structural reform to unregulated private enterprise. The aid and reform were not as dramatic as supporters or critics of the New Deal claimed. African-American communities were the hardest hit and received the least amount of relief.

Standardized Tests and Tracking

These racial divisions were especially evident in American schooling. By the early 1920s, standardized IQ tests were being used to track millions of students into separate educational curricula. Lewis Terman of Stanford University first developed these tests for schools. The questions on the test were based on a small norm-referenced sample of white, middle- and upper-class children and adults. Terman, like most other white educational researchers of the day, believed these tests objectively measured aptitude and could be used by school systems to rank, order, and sort the school-age population of America. The use of these tests in this fashion reflected a eugenic ideology of human worth, where some individuals and groups were born to be superior and others fated to be inferior. (See article, page 76)

African-American children were routinely channeled into either low tracks or separate vocational schools based upon low scores on IQ tests. The resources, curricula, and instruction African-American students received reflected the lower academic expectations white school officials had for them. Unsurprisingly, this institutional racism contributed to high rates of failure and poor school performance among many African-American students. White teachers of African–American students frequently assumed it was the "low mental level" of the race that accounted for their problems in school. [2]

W.E.B. DuBois with Mary McLeod Bethune and Horace Mann Bond in 1950 after receiving Lincoln University's Medallion Awards.

The mainstream academic community had given legitimacy to these attitudes in the 1920s. The use of testing for racial tracking purposes had been supported and promoted by distinguished educational theorists. Carl Brigham, Assistant Professor of Psychology at Princeton University, wrote one of the most influential racist interpretations of the IQ test at the time. His book, *A Study of American Intelligence*, was widely read by policymakers, educators, and the general public. It was frequently referred to in testimony given before the House Immigration hearings. The book provided a "scientific" rationale for the racist quotas established in the 1924 immigration act.

Brigham would later become a dean at Princeton and go on to develop the Scholastic Aptitude Test (SAT). In *A Study of American Intelligence* he wrote:

> According to all evidence available then, American intelligence is declining, and will proceed with an accelerating rate as the racial admixture becomes more and more extensive. The decline of American intelligence will be more rapid than the decline of the intelligence of European groups, owing to the presence here of the negro. These are the plain, if somewhat ugly, facts that our study shows. [3]

His book had a monumental impact on public policy and schooling. This book, along with numerous other educational publications in the 1920s, provided the intellectual rationale for inferior schools and diminished educational expectations for African-American students.

While Brigham's ideas represented a dominant educational ideology of the 1920s, these beliefs would not go unchallenged. Helping to lead that challenge were African-American social

scientists and educators. They would expose the false assumptions and faulty methodology of those who claimed the tests proved "Negro inferiority." In doing so, they would open up a more expansive vision of intelligence and learning.

The Role of Black Colleges

The wellspring for resistance began in the Black colleges of the era. These institutions were established in the mid-19th century when African-American men and women were denied admission into White universities. The situation had not changed greatly by the 1920s. By 1940 there were more than 100 Black colleges in operation. Though inadequately funded, understaffed, and with limited facilities, these colleges nonetheless played a vital role in training the men and women who provided counter arguments to the use of tests for tracking and racial ranking. [4]

This was not an easy thing to do in the early 20th century. Most of the academics generating studies on IQ testing were trained in doctoral programs in psychology. Only a few northern universities accepted African-American students into doctoral psychology programs. Black colleges in the 1920s were just beginning to offer doctorates in this field. It was even more difficult for African-American women to get graduate level training in psychology in this era.

Despite these challenges, the Black colleges offered a unique educational environment, one that nurtured a different view of human potential. White researchers in the area of human development throughout the 1920s usually focused on the differences among human beings. Educators at these Black colleges stressed the inherent similarities. [5]

African-American scholars who graduated from these schools also challenged the accepted myths that were held as scientific truth by most of their White counterparts. These included:

■ Test scores proved that African-Americans and other "lesser strains" were innately inferior to Northern European Whites.

■ Environmental conditions had little to do with performance on IQ tests. Intelligence was essentially fixed and unchangeable.

■ Exceptionally intelligent children were rarely found among African–Americans.

■ Children of mixed White and Black ancestry had a higher intelligence than "pure Negro" Blacks. (This was known as the "mulatto hypothesis" at the time.)

■ Better educational opportunities made little difference in helping children succeed.

One of the first educators to challenge these myths and Brigham's interpretations of IQ test scores was Horace Mann Bond (1904-1972). Bond wrote a scathing critique of "A Study of American Intelligence in Crisis," the official magazine of the NAACP. Bond, like other African-American intellectuals of the era, found it very difficult to be published in the white-controlled press. Publications like "Crisis" and "The Journal of Negro Education" were crucial in circulating the ideas of African-American writers.

His article, "Intelligence Tests and Propaganda" was published in 1924. At the time Bond was the Director of the School of Education at Langston University in Oklahoma. While not formally trained as a psychologist, Bond demonstrated a remarkable insight into the construction and use of these tests. In the article he dismissed the claim that these tests were objective. Instead, Bond called them "funds for propaganda" and encouraged each African-American student to:

> ... be in possession of every detail of the operation, use, and origin of these tests, in order that he might better equip himself as an active agent against the insidious propaganda which seeks to demonstrate that the Negro is intellectually and physically incapable of assuming the dignities, rights, and duties which devolve upon him as a member of modern society. [6]

> *The past can have a remarkable power to persist. The Bell Curve, a bestseller in the 1990s, recycles arguments debunked in the 1920s.*

Bond went on to model what he hoped inquiring students would do with this kind of research. In particular, he questioned Brigham's thesis, which was widely shared by psychological testers, that African Americans from the North who scored consistently better on IQ tests did so because they were a "higher strain of Negro." Bond drew attention to the fact that African-American children on average received relatively better education in northern schools than their counterparts in the South.

Bond offered a small study he conducted among college freshmen at Lincoln University to refute Brigham's thesis. The number of African-American students from Northern and Southern states was about evenly divided at the school. Bond administered IQ tests similar to the ones used on U.S. Army recruits and subsequently analyzed by Brigham in *A Study in American Intelligence*. Bond discovered that students from the South did not do as well on these tests as Northern students. Unlike Brigham his study demonstrated that the resources, preparation of the teaching staff, and curricula were worse in the Jim Crow schools of the South. Bond wrote that academic performance of these students at Lincoln did improve when given better opportunities. He wrote:

> When placed in the same environment, given the same treatment, taught by the same staff, it is found that these men from the poorer Southern schools are just as quick in grasping and making the best of the new college surroundings. [7]

Other African-American educators at this time, such as Howard Hale Long of Paine College, raised similar objections to Brigham's work. Their writings and Bond's research did not receive any outside foundation funding nor were they widely reported. Yet, Bond highlighted some of the underlying causes for variations in test scores between different groups of students. Since his time, hundreds of better-funded research studies have confirmed his essential premises.

Attacking IQ Myths

In 1927 Bond wrote another article in "Crisis." In this essay, Bond attacked the myth that IQ test scores proved African-Americans had no people of "exceptional intellect." Bond's tone was impatient and filled with sarcasm as he referred to IQ testing as a "major indoor sport among psychologists."[8] He wondered why White psychologists emphasized the need for a rapport between White testers and white children but did not think it necessary to emphasize the same approach with African-American children. He also wondered why normed samples were always based on White middle- and upper-class students.

Bond and his research team decided to "alter the rules of the game." They were determined to create a positive and reassuring environment for the students chosen to take the test. They also wanted to include students from a variety of economic backgrounds. Thirty school children from Chicago were selected for the study. A comfortable testing situation was provided in a small group setting. Students were given encouragement and emotional support before the test was administered. The students came from working-class, middle-class, and professional family backgrounds.

The results of the test shattered long standing beliefs in the testing community. Bond found that 63% of the children scored above 106, whereas Terman found in his sample of White youth that only 33% did so. Bond added, "Mr. Terman states that only 5% of White children may be expected to equal or exceed an IQ of 122; no less than 47% of our subjects exceeded this score."[9] Bond was not making the case for a reverse racial superiority. Rather he argued that economic class, parental emphasis of reading at an early age, and a stimulating school environment would boost scores for all children.

By 1930 most research into differences in intelligence had moved away from racial explanations. While racist social attitudes and polices were still entrenched in the larger society, African-American researchers were now joined by a few prominent White colleagues. The published works by anthropologist Melville Herskovits and psychologist Otto Klineberg in the 1930s supported the findings of Bond. They were some of the first White social scientists, along with Franz Boas and Margaret Mead, to write and speak out against the racial myths infusing the research on intelligence testing.

Ansell Horn/Impact Visuals

Also, in the 1930s African-American intellectuals were beginning to receive more opportunities to publish and gain resources for extensive research studies. The playing field was hardly equal, but these scholars took advantage of the small openings that appeared. This can be seen in the work of Martin Jenkins (1904-1978). Jenkins did his undergraduate work at Howard University and was the first African-American to receive a Ph.D. in psychology from Northwestern University, in 1935. He built upon the work of Bond and others in the 1920s to do major studies of school children in Chicago.

Jenkins confirmed what people like Bond and Long had been saying in the 1920s. He found that a greater percentage of African-American students scored higher on IQ tests when they had elevated economic and educational backgrounds. Furthermore, these scores were represented evenly throughout various age and grade levels, as long as students maintained higher levels of economic and educational support. No evidence supported the thesis that African-American students who performed well on the tests did so because of alleged White ancestry. Jenkins conclusions were clear:

The findings of this study suggest that the differences in test performance of white and Negro children found by so many investigators are not due to inherent racial factors ... In home background, in developmental history, in physical development, in school progress, in educational achievement, in interests, in activities, and in social and personal characteristics, Negro children of superior intelligence [high scores on IQ tests] resemble other American children of superior intelligence.[10]

Jenkins was able to cite numerous studies by both Black and White educators in drawing his conclusions. Also, now he and other African-American scholars were beginning to be cited by White scholars such as Herskovitz and Klineberg. New ground was being broken. In 1939 Jenkins was one of the first African-American researchers to have his findings about race and IQ included in an educational journal that was not restricted to primarily African-American audiences. Previously, articles of this kind had to be co-authored with a White scholar if they were to be accepted in publications such as *The Journal of Educational Psychology* or *The Journal of Social Psychology*.

Many other African-American scholars also spoke out and wrote against the racist use of IQ tests. Herman Canady, Charles St. Clair Price, and Charles Johnson were only some of the names.[11] They represented varying interests in approaching questions of race and IQ testing. Yet almost all entered their research with a basic assumption that students were similar in their capacity to achieve when provided with adequate learning environments and social opportunities.

The Legacy for Today

The legacy of these efforts is with us today. Progressive education rests on some of the foundation blocks laid by people like Horace Mann Bond and Martin Jenkins. Many of today's educational programs have sprung from their contributions. The need for early intervention programs in reading, the importance of using multiple assessments to monitor student learning, and the need to create school cultures that foster high expectations for all students are beliefs that have been drawn from their work. They make up the canon of good education. However, when African-American educators were writing in the '20s their ideas often were seen as radical, flying in the face of established dogma.

Also, we know that discredited ideas from the past can have a remarkable power to persist. It is

a terrible irony that Charles Murray and Richard Herrnstein's *The Bell Curve*, the modern day equivalent of Carl Brigham's *A Study in American Intelligence*, is more well-known than the writings of Bond or Jenkins. And it is a scandal that *The Bell Curve* recycles some of the arguments debunked by African-American intellectuals back in the 1920s but still manages to become a best seller in the 1990s.

Brigham recanted his views in 1930 because he realized that the findings of Bond, Jenkins, Long, Klineberg, and others undermined the credibility of his work. Brigham concluded in his article in *The Psychological Review*:

> This review has summarized some of the most recent test findings which show that comparative studies of various national and racial groups may not be made with existing tests, and which show, in particular, that one of the most pretentious of these comparative racial studies — the writer's own — was without foundation.[12]

No such recantation has ever come from Herrnstein, now deceased, or Murray.

While still embraced by some policymakers and academics, The Bell Curve has also been denounced by a range of scholars and lay people — quite a different reaction from when Brigham's A Study in American Intelligence was published. This time many White educators joined African-American scholars in writing and speaking out against the assumptions, methodology, and policy conclusions found in the book. The nearly forgotten graduates of Howard, Lincoln, Virginia Union, and numerous other Black colleges had laid the intellectual foundations for these critiques much earlier.

As things change, they remain the same. Jim Crow no longer rules American society. The views of Terman and Brigham on race and intelligence would be on the margins of today's educational research. But we also know that attitudes and practices of the past can be reworked and institutionalized in other ways. In fact, the echoes of the past are loudly heard in the reliance on high-stakes tests to shape educational policy. Except now the tests are not purporting to be sorting devices based on a racial ranking according to IQ scores but instead on student, teacher, and school performance. The schools and students who do poorly on these

> *White researchers in the 1920's focused on the differences among people.*
> *Black educators stressed the similitaries.*

Kathy Sloane

exams will once again be those who do not have access to better resources. The tracking and unequal funding that were institutionalized in the 1920s will be only further entrenched in the current incarnation of high-stakes testing.

The past efforts of African-American educators can be instructive for the educational climate we are living in today. Black colleges helped nurture an alternative paradigm to intelligence and learning that enabled African-American educators to question the dominant assumptions of the day. Today we need educational spaces in our communities that encourage similar alternative views to established policy. In the 1920s and '30s African-American educators struggled against incredible racial barriers. Their ideas deserved a wider circulation. Today, we have greater opportunities to build coalitions with various groups of people to press for a rethinking of what is being accepted as dogma.

Equally important is the contribution these educators made in keeping alive the promise of American democracy. When schools mimicked the policies of exclusion in the wider society, African-American intellectuals demanded a higher standard of democratic justice for the nation's youth. Through moral outrage and intellectual rigor they helped set in motion a movement of ideas that defined education as the liberation of human potential. Those ideas were needed then. We must not forget them today. ❏

— Alan Stoskopf (Alan Stoskopf@Facing.org) is Associate Program Director for Facing History and Ourselves. The views expressed in this article are solely the author's.

The above is reprinted from Rethinking Schools, Vol. 14, #1, Fall 1999.

FOR FURTHER READING

V. P. Franklin, "Black Social Scientists and the Mental Testing Movement, 1920-1940," in Reginald L. Jones, ed., Black Psychology, 3rd ed. (Berkeley: Cobb & Henry, 1991).

Robert V. Guthrie, Even the Rat Was White: A Historical View of Psychology, 2nd ed. (Boston: Allyn and Bacon, 1998).

Sandra Harding, ed., The Racial Economy of Science: Toward a Democratic Future (Bloomington: Indiana University Press, 1993).

FOOTNOTES

[1] As quoted in Robert V. Guthrie, *Even the Rat Was White: A Historical View of Psychology* (2nd edition) (Boston: Allyn & Bacon, 1998), p. 55.

[2] David Tyack, *The One Best System* (Cambridge: Harvard University Press, 1974), p. 219.

[3] Carl Brigham, *A Study in American Intelligence* (Princeton: Princeton University Press, 1923), p. 210.

[4] Guthrie, p. 123.

[5] Ibid., p. 125.

[6] Horace Mann Bond, "Intelligence Tests and Propaganda," *The Crisis*, vol. 28(2), June, 1924, p. 61.

[7] Ibid., p. 63.

[8] Horace Mann Bond, "Some Exceptional Negro Children," *The Crisis*, vol. 34(8), October, 1927, p. 257.

[9] Ibid., p. 259.

[10] Martin D. Jenkins, "A Socio-Psychological Study of Negro Children of Superior Intelligence," vol. 5 (2), April 1936, pp. 189-190.

[11] See bibliography of V. P. Franklin, "Black Social Scientists and the Mental Testing Movement, 1920-1940," in *Black Psychology*, 3rd ed., pp. 222-224.

[12] Carl Brigham, "Intelligence Traits of Immigrant Groups," *The Psychological Review XXXVII* (1930), p. 165.

Standards and Multiculturalism

Multiculturalism is a search, a conversation to discover silenced perspectives. Yet standards emphasize one 'fixed' answer.

BY BILL BIGELOW

Proponents of "higher standards" and more testing promise raised expectations for all students and increased "accountability." In practice, their reforms are hostile to good teaching and pose a special threat to multiculturalism.

The state where I teach, Oregon, has joined the national testing craze. This fall the Oregon Department of Education field-tested its first-ever statewide social studies assessments. Many teachers were dismayed to discover that the tests were a multiple-choice maze that lurched about helter-skelter, seeking answers on World War I, Constitutional amendments, global climate, rivers in India, hypothetical population projections, Supreme Court decisions, and economic terminology. Evidently, for the state of Oregon, social studies knowledge is little more than acquiring piles of disconnected facts about the world.

If it prevails, Oregon's brand of standardization will undermine a multicultural curriculum — one that describes and attempts to explain the world as it really exists; speaks to the diversity of our society and our students; and aims not only to teach important facts, but to develop citizens who can make the world safer and more just.

In a sense, the entire effort to create fixed standards violates the very essence of multiculturalism. Multiculturalism is, in the words of Harvard professor Henry Louis Gates Jr., a search, a "conversation among different voices," to discover perspectives that have been silenced in traditional scholastic narratives. Multiculturalism attempts to uncover "the histories and experiences of people who have been left out of the curriculum," as anti-racist educator Enid Lee emphasizes. Because multiculturalism is an undertaking that requires new scholarship and constant discussion, it necessarily is ongoing. Yet as researcher Harold Berlak points out in the Spring issue of *Rethinking Schools*, "standardization and centralization of curriculum testing is an effort to put an end to a cacophony of voices on what constitutes truth, knowledge, and learning and what the young should be taught. It insists upon one set of answers." Curriculum standardization is, as Berlak indicates, a way to silence dissident voices, "a way to manufacture consent and cohesion."

Creating official, government-approved social studies standards is bound to be controversial, whether at the national or state level. Thus, according to the Portland Oregonian, state education officials "tried to stake a neutral ground," in order to win approval for its version of social reality. "We have tried so hard to go right down the middle between what teachers want, what parents want, and what the [Republican-dominated] Legislature wants," according to Dawn Billings, a Department of Education curriculum coordinator. Not surprisingly, this attempt to be "neutral" and inoffensive means that the standards lack a critical sensibility — an emphasis on conflict and diversity of interpretation — and tend towards a conservative Father Knows Best portrait of history and society. For example, one typical tenth-grade benchmark calls for students to "understand how the Constitution can be a vehicle for change and for resolving issues as well as a device for preserving values and principles of society."

Is this how, say, Frederick Douglass or the Seminole leader, Osceola, would have seen the Constitution? Shouldn't students also understand how the Constitution can be (and has been) a

> *Multicultural education does not just impart lots of interesting facts, but equips students to transform the world.*

vehicle for preserving class and race stratification and for maintaining the privileges of dominant social groups? For example, in the 1857 Dred Scott case, the Supreme Court held that a slave could not sue for his freedom because he was property, not a human being. Chief Justice Roger Taney declared that no Black person in the United States had "any rights which the White man is bound to respect." The Abolitionist William Lloyd Garrison called the Constitution an "agreement with Hell" for its support of slavery. And in 1896 the Supreme Court ruled in Plessy v. Ferguson that segregation — "separate but equal" — did not violate the Fourteenth Amendment.

Constitutional Realities

Almost 40% of the men who wrote the Constitution owned slaves, including George Washington and James Madison. In my U.S. history classes

we look at the adoption of the Constitution from the standpoint of poor White farmers, enslaved African-Americans, unemployed workers in urban areas, and other groups. Students create their own Constitution in a mock assembly, and then compare their document to the actual Constitution. They discover, for example, that the Constitution does not include the word "slave" but instead refers euphemistically to enslaved African-Americans, as in Article 4, Section 2: "No person held to service or labor in one state, under the laws thereof, escaping into another, shall in consequence of any law or regulation therein, be discharged from such service or labor, but shall be delivered up on claim of the party to whom such service or labor may be due." It's a vicious clause that sits uncomfortably in the "preserving values and principles" rhetoric of Oregon's standards.

It is probably inevitable that school curricula

ORGANIZATIONAL POSITION

Appropriate Use of Tests

The following is from a recent report by The National Research Council of the National Academy of Sciences. The section below, taken from the Executive Summary, deals with basic principles of appropriately using tests. The report, "High Stakes: Testing for Tracking, Promotion, and Graduation," is available at www.nap.edu.

■ The important thing about a test is not its validity in general, but its validity when used for a specific purpose. Thus, tests that are valid for influencing classroom practice, "leading" the curriculum, or holding schools accountable aren't appropriate for making high-stakes decisions about individual student mastery unless the curriculum, the teaching, and the test[s] are aligned.

■ Tests are not perfect. Test questions are a sample of possible questions that could be asked in a given area. Moreover, a test score is not an exact measure of a student's knowledge or skills. A student's score can be expected to vary across different versions of a test — within a margin of error determined by the reliability of the test — as a function of the particular sample of questions asked and/or transitory factors, such as the student's health on the day of the test. Thus, no single test score can be considered a definitive measure of a student's knowledge.

■ An educational decision that will have a major impact on a test-taker should not be made solely or automatically on the basis of a single test score. Other relevant information about the student's knowledge and skills should also be taken into account.

■ Neither a test score nor any other kind of information can justify a bad decision. Research shows that students are typically hurt by simple retention and repetition of a grade in school without remedial and other instructional support services. In the absence of effective services for low-performing students, better tests will not lead to better educational outcomes.

will reflect the contradictions between a society's myths and realities. But while a critical multicultural approach attempts to examine these contradictions, standardization tends to paper them over. For example, another benchmark — "Explain how laws are developed and applied to provide order, set limits, protect basic rights, and promote the common good" — similarly fails the multicultural test. Whose order, whose basic rights, are protected by laws? Are all social groups included equally in the term "common good?" Between 1862 and 1890, laws in the United States gave 180,000,000 acres (an area the size of Texas and Oklahoma) to privately-owned railroad companies, but gave virtually no land to African– Americans freed from slavery in the South. Viewing the Constitution and other U.S. laws through a multicultural lens would add texture and depth to the facile one-sidedness of Oregon's "neutral" standards.

Indeed the "R" word, racism, is not mentioned once in any of the seven 1998 11th-grade field tests nor in the social studies standards adopted in March 1998 by the State Board of Education. Even if the only yardstick were strict historical accuracy this would be a bizarre omission: the state was launched as a Whites-only territory by the Oregon Donation Act and in racist wars of dispossession waged against indigenous peoples; the first constitution outlawed slavery but also forbade Blacks from living in the state, a prohibition that remained on the books until 1926. Perhaps state education officials are concerned that introducing the concept of racism to students could call into question the essentially harmonious world of "change and continuity over time" that underpins the standards project. Whatever the reason, there is no way that students can make sense of the world today without the idea of racism in their conceptual knapsack. If a key goal of multiculturalism is to account for how the past helped shape the present, and an important part of the present is social inequality, then Oregon's standards and tests earn a failing grade.

Despite the publication of state social studies standards and benchmarks, teachers and parents don't really know what students are expected to

Rick Reinharfd

learn until they see the tests, which were developed by an out-of-state assessment corporation, MetriTech. As Prof. Wade W. Nelson points out in a delightfully frank article, "The Naked Truth about School Reform in Minnesota" (that might as well have been written about Oregon), "The content of the standards is found only in the tests used to assess them. Access to the tests themselves is carefully controlled, making it difficult to get a handle on what these standards are. It seems ironic to me that basic standards — that which every student is expected to know or be able to do — are revealed only in tests accessible only to test-makers and administrators. This design avoids much of the debate about what these standards ought to be" — a debate which is essential to the ongoing struggle for a multicultural curriculum.

Discrete Facts

It's when you look directly at the tests that their limitations and negative implications for multiculturalism become most clear. Test questions inevitably focus on discrete facts, but cannot address the deeper, multi-faceted meaning of facts. For example, in the field tests Oregon piloted in the fall of 1998, one question asked which Constitutional Amendment gave women the right to vote. Students could know virtually nothing about the long struggle for women's rights and get this question right. On the other hand, they could know lots about the feminist movement and not recall that it was the 19th and not the 16th, 17th, or 18th Amendment (the other test choices) that gave women the right to vote.

Because there is no way to predict precisely which facts will be sought on the state tests, teachers will feel pressured to turn courses into a "memory Olympics;" teachers simply could not afford to spend time probing beneath the headlines of history.

Last year, my students at Franklin High School in Portland performed a role play on the 1848 Seneca Falls, NY, women's rights conference, the first formal U.S. gathering to demand greater equality for women. The original assembly was composed largely of middle- to upper-class White women. I wanted my students to appreciate the issues that these women addressed and their courage, but also to consider the limitations imposed by their race, class, and ethnicity. Thus in our simulated 1848 gathering, my students portrayed women who were not at the original conference — enslaved African–Americans, Cherokee women who had been forcibly moved to Oklahoma on the Trail of Tears, Mexican women in the recently conquered territory of New Mexico, poor White New England mill workers — as well as the White middle- and upper-class reformers like Elizabeth Cady Stanton and Lucretia Mott who were in attendance.

In this more socially representative fictional assembly, students learned about the resolutions adopted at the original gathering and the conditions that motivated those, but they also saw first-hand how more privileged White women ignored other important issues such as treaty rights of Mexican women, sexual abuse of enslaved African-Americans, and the workplace exploitation of poor White women, that a more diverse convention might have addressed.

The knowledge that my students acquired from this role play consisted not only of "facts" — although they learned plenty of these. They also

> *At its core, multicultural teaching is an ethical, even political, enterprise. It has heart and soul.*

exercised their multicultural social imaginations — listening for the voices that are often silenced in the traditional U.S. history narrative, becoming more alert to the importance of issues of race and class. However, this kind of teaching and learning takes time — time that could be ill-afforded in the fact-packing pedagogy required by multiple-choice tests. And after all their study, would my students have recalled whether it was the 16th, 17th, 18th, or 19th Amendment that gave women the right to vote? If not, they would have appeared ignorant about the struggle for women's rights.

Likewise, my Global Studies students spend the better part of a quarter reading, discussing, role-playing, and writing about the manifold consequences of European colonialism. They read excerpts from Okot p'Bitek's poignant book-length poem, *Song of Lawino*, about the lingering psychological effects of colonialism in Uganda; role play a trial on the colonial roots of the potato famine in Ireland; and examine how Asian economies were distorted to serve the needs of European ruling classes. But when confronted with Oregon's multiple-choice question that asks which continent was most thoroughly colonized in 1914, would my students answer correctly?

As these examples illustrate, in a multicultural curriculum it's not so much facts as it is perspective that is important in nurturing a fuller understanding of society. And sometimes considering new perspectives requires imagination as much as or more than memory of specific facts. For example, my history students read about the people Columbus encountered in 1492, the Taínos — who themselves left no written records — in excerpts from Columbus's journal and articles like Jose Barriero's "Taínos: Men of the Good." I ask students to write a story or diary entry from the point of view of a Taíno during the first few days or weeks of their encounter with Spaniards that draws on information in the readings, but goes further. It's necessarily a speculative undertaking, but invites students to turn the "Columbus discovers America" story on its head, encourages them to appreciate the humanity in the people usually marginalized in tales of "exploration." In response, students have written pieces of startling insight. Sure, a multiple choice test can assess whether students know that

Jean-Claude Lejeune

Columbus first sailed in 1492, where he landed, or the name of the people he encountered. But it is ill-equipped to assess what students truly understand about this encounter.

Not surprisingly, Oregon's "one best answer" approach vastly over-simplifies and misrepresents complex social processes — and entirely erases ethnicity and race as categories of analysis. One question on a recent test reads: "In 1919, over 4.1 million Americans belonged to labor unions. By 1928, that number had dropped to 3.4 million. Which of the following best accounts for that drop?" It seems that the correct answer must be A. "Wages increased dramatically, so workers didn't need unions." All the other answers are clearly wrong, but is this answer "correct"? Since when do workers leave unions when they win higher wages? Weren't mechanization and scientific management factors in undermining traditional craft unions? Did the post-World War I Red Scare, with systematic attacks on radical unions like the Industrial Workers of the World and deportations of foreign-born labor organizers affect union membership?

And how about the Oregon test's reductive category of "worker"? Shouldn't students be alert to how race, ethnicity, and gender were and are important factors in determining one's workplace experience, including union membership? For example, in 1919, professional strikebreakers, hired by steel corporations, were told to "stir up as much bad feeling as you possibly can between the Serbians and the Italians." And more than 30,000 Black workers, excluded from AFL unions, were brought in as strikebreakers. A multicultural awareness is vital if we're to arrive at a satisfactory answer to the above Oregon field-test question. But the state would reward students for choosing an historical sound-bite that is as shallow as it is wrong.

This leads me to an aspect of these tests that is especially offensive to teachers: they don't merely assess, they also instruct. The tests represent the authority of the state, implicitly telling students, "Just memorize the facts, kids. That's what social studies is all about — and if teachers do any more than that, they're wasting your time." Multiple-choice tests undermine teachers' efforts to construct a rigorous multicultural curriculum because they delegitimate that curriculum in students' eyes: If it were important it would be on the test.

Core of Multiculturalism

At its core, multicultural teaching is an ethical, even political, enterprise. Its aim is not just to impart lots of interesting facts, to equip students to be proficient Trivial Pursuit players, but to help make the world a better place. It highlights injustice of all kinds — racial, gender, class, linguistic, ethnic, national, environmental — in order to make explanations and propose solutions. It recognizes our responsibility to fellow human beings and to the earth. It has heart and soul.

Compare that with the sterile, fact-collecting orientation of Oregon's standards and assessments. For example, a typical 49-question high-school field test piloted in 1998 included seven questions on global climate, two on the location of rivers in India and Africa, and one on hypothetical world population projections in the year 2050. But not a single question in the test concerned the lives of people around the world, or environmental conditions — nothing about increasing poverty, the global AIDS epidemic, disappearance of the rain forests, rates of unemployment, global warming, etc., or efforts to address these crises. The test bounded aimlessly from one disjointed fact to another. In the most profound sense it was pointless.

Indeed the test's random amorality may reveal another of its cultural biases. Oregon's standards and assessments make no distinction between knowledge and information. The state's version of social education would appear to have no raison d'être beyond the acquisition of large quantities of data. But for many cultures, the aim of knowledge is not bulk, but wisdom — insight into meaningful aspects about the nature of life. Writing in the winter 1998/1999 *Rethinking Schools*, Peter Kiang makes a similar point about the Massachusetts teacher test that calls into question the validity of enterprises such as these. He writes that "by constructing a test based on a sequence of isolated, decontextualized questions that have no relationship to each other, the underlying epistemology embedded in the test design has a Western-cultural bias, even if individual questions include or represent 'multicultural' content. Articulating and assessing a knowledge base requires examining not only what one knows, but also how one knows."

Students "know" in different ways, and these differences are often cultural. Oregon nonetheless subjects all students to an abstract, data-heavy assessment device that does not gauge what or how they have learned. As Kiang points out, test-makers address multicultural criticism by including individual questions about multicultural content — for example, by highlighting snippets of information about famous people of color like Martin Luther King Jr., Cesar Chavez, and Harriet Tubman. But these "heroes and holidays" additions cannot mask the fundamental hostility to multicultural education shown by standards and assessments like those initiated by Oregon.

Spelling out an alternative to Oregon's culturally biased, superficial "accountability" plan would require another article. In brief, I want the state to abandon its effort to turn me into a delivery system of approved social information. I want it to support me and other teachers as we collaborate to create curriculum that deals forthrightly with social problems, that fights racism and social injustice. I want it to support teachers as we construct rigorous performance standards for students that promote deep thinking about the nature of our society. I want it to acknowledge the legitimacy of a multicultural curriculum of critical questions, complexity, multiple perspectives, and social imagination. I want it to admit that wisdom is more than information — that the world can't be chopped up into multiple-choice questions, and that you can't bubble-in the truth with a number-two pencil. ❐

> ## QUOTABLE QUOTE
>
> "The question, for me, isn't if we ought to have some 'standards' in our children's education. It is, rather, how and where they are determined, and by whom, and how they're introduced, and how we treat or penalize (or threaten, or abuse) the child or the teacher who won't swallow them."
>
> — *Jonathan Kozol, from the introduction to Deborah Meier's book, Will Standards Save Public Education?*

— *Bill Bigelow (bbpdx@aol.com) teaches at Franklin High School in Portland, OR, and is an editor of Rethinking Schools. The Oregon Department of Education has threatened that teachers can be fired for writing about test questions — even those that appear on "pilot" tests. Thus, for safety considerations, the questions described here are the same as those that were included in Bigelow's article, "Tests From Hell," in Rethinking Schools, Vol. 13, #2, Winter 1998/1999.*

The above appeared in Rethinking Schools, Vol. 13, #4, Summer 1999. A version of this article first appeared in Educational Leadership, April 1999.

Standards and the Control of Knowledge

What will be the impact of state-mandated standards and tests on efforts to forge a truly multicultural curriculum?

BY HAROLD BERLAK

State-mandated standards and tests by design visit on teachers and students a particular and singular view of the "basics" of history, geography, literature, art, and ways of looking at and thinking about truth. They are an effort to put an end to the most valuable asset of a multicultural society: its vibrant cacophony of views about what constitutes truth, knowledge, and learning, and about what young children ought and ought not to learn at school. Standardized curriculum and tests insist upon one set of answers, and only one.

While standardized testing and rankings by test score have long been a part of the educational landscape, the effort to install national tests and reliance on statewide standardized testing is now on an entirely unprecedented scale. This major shift in national and state educational policy was initiated during the presidency of George Bush.

Lamar Alexander, Bush's Secretary of Education and former Republican governor of Tennessee, sought and received Congressional authorization to create a commission to study the feasibility of establishing national educational standards tied to testing. That report, *Raising Standards for American Education*, arrived on Jan. 24, 1992, and marked the beginning of this latest effort to shift curriculum decisions away from local authorities, schools, and teachers toward centralized, bureaucratic state control. Now, more than ever, the major issues of what and how to teach are being decided by politicians, government agencies such as the National Goals Panel, state legislatures, state boards of education, and a raft of appointed committees, panels, and commissions.

That tests are intended to mandate control of the culture is not a controversial claim. The architects of these policies proclaim it. The 1992 report, *Raising Standards for American Education*, asserts that national educational standards would "bind together a wide variety of groups into one

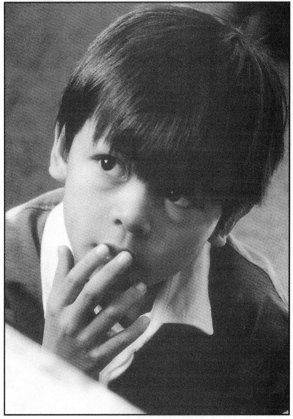

Jean-Claude Lejeune

nation," providing "shared values and knowledge" which will serve "as a powerful force for national unity." Lauren Resnick, a chief academic advocate for testing and a former president of the American Educational Research Association, argued, *"Without performance standards, the meaning of content standards is subject to interpretation, which if allowed to vary would undermine efforts to set high standards for the majority of American students."* (Italics added.)

Reinforcing the Dominant Culture

Linking standards and curriculum to high-stakes testing is a powerful and pervasive way to ensure the continued hegemony of the dominant culture. Or, to use the more apt language of

Edward Said, the distinguished Palestinian-American scholar, it is a late 20th century form of cultural imperialism.

It is not coincidental that the concerted effort by government authorities to gain monopoly control over the curriculum arrives at the time that social movements have appeared and are challenging male, White Anglo-European political and cultural supremacy. The formerly enslaved, colonized, and oppressed do not accept their ascribed cultural, racial, and gender inferiority. Many are asserting their rights to reclaim cultural power, and to create and forge their own cultural and social identities.

For those who see these movements as cultural balkanization and a threat to social order, standardization and centralization of curriculum and testing serve both as an antidote to the demand for greater cultural diversity and as a way to manufacture consent and maintain the dominant culture. They serve to reduce what they perceive as a threat: multiculturalists, anti-racists, feminists, and others whom they fear are sowing seeds of disunity, threatening the fabric of the nation.

What they overlook, however, is that although movements for cultural, racial, and gender equality and justice can be temporarily contained and diverted, they cannot be extinguished. The genie will not return to the bottle. The root issues remain race, culture, class, gender, and, of course, power.

Thus centralized testing is enmeshed in the so-called "culture wars," or, to give it a proper name, the multiculturalism question. Multiculturalism is not primarily about the content of the canon — whose literature, history, ideas of art, music, and ways of thinking are to be included and excluded in the mandated curriculum and in the tests (important as this may be). Rather, multiculturalism at its core is about who has the power to decide. Put another way, a state-mandated multicultural curriculum is an oxymoron, since the power to decide remains with the culturally and politically dominant groups that control state government. ❐

— *Harold Berlak is a university teacher, independent scholar, and educational activist living in Oakland, CA. He is the author of several books and articles dealing with curriculum, pedagogy, educational policy, and assessment. He is also among the founding members of the National Coalition of Educational Activists.*

© 1999 Harold Berlak. Significant portions of this article are adapted from a chapter in the book Assessment: Social Practice and Social Product, Ann Filer, ed. (London: Falmer Press, 1999).

The above article is excerpted from Rethinking Schools, Vol. 13, #3, Spring 1999. The full text is available online at www.rethinkingschools.org, go to "Past Issues."

Kirk Anderson

FAILING OUR KIDS:
WHY THE TESTING CRAZE WON'T FIX OUR SCHOOLS

Alternatives to Standardized Testing

Alternatives to Standardized Tests

There's only one thing as bad as requiring students to reduce all learning to a single 'correct' answer, and that is reducing assessment and accountability to a single standardized test.

BY BOB PETERSON AND MONTY NEILL

Critics of standardized tests are often asked, "What's your alternative?" It's a legitimate — and important — question. Parents and community members have the right to know how well their children are learning.

Unfortunately, in part due to rhetoric that equates high standards with standardized tests, many parents believe that standardized tests will give them the answer. At the same time, parents are often the first to understand that the complexity of their child cannot be captured by a test score.

At issue is how to create replacements for standardized tests that will inform parents and community members about how well the schools are doing and whether their children are learning what they need to know — that is, how to create an alternative approach to accountability.

Teachers assess students regularly as part of their on-going teaching. The challenge is to match assessment that is integrated into classroom instruction, and is focused primarily on helping individual children, with assessment that provides school- and district-wide information being demanded by local and state officials or various community forces.

One of the first steps toward rethinking assessments is to ask, "What is the purpose of the assessment?" and, "Is this purpose worthy or meaningful?" Answering these questions means addressing what is important for students to learn, how we help them learn, and how we know what they have learned.

Too often, the rationale for standardized testing appears overly punitive: "We're going to get these kids and schools to perform better — or else." Such an approach forgets that assessment should serve one primary purpose: to provide information to help the student learn better.

Assessment serves other purposes as well. Community members may want data to see if schools are providing equal opportunity to all students. Policy-makers might want to know the effectiveness of various programs. Districts and state legislatures want to see how well the schools are spending taxpayers' money. Schools want a way to report to parents, or summarize and certify a student's achievement. Finally, districts might use changes in assessment policy to help transform the curriculum.

Depending on the purpose, different forms of assessment might be used. For example, an assessment designed to evaluate how well a school, overall, is teaching its students to read should not be used to decide whether a particular student should or should not be promoted to fourth grade.

Alternatives to standardized testing are in use in both the United States and other industrialized countries. The alternatives range from student portfolios, to district-wide "proficiencies," to outside review teams that evaluate a school. There is growing evidence that these measures do a better job of showing how well students and schools are performing.

The biggest drawback to most alternatives is that they challenge this country's predominant approach to thinking and learning — that is, that we can only truly know something if it can be statistically and "objectively" determined and analyzed.

Alternative assessments require diversity in thinking about what is the purpose of knowledge and, indeed, even what constitutes knowledge. To challenge statistical ways of knowing is to challenge the status quo and its tendency to marginalize and describe as abnormal those who do not neatly fit into a statistical box. Alternative assessments mean alternative voices, perspectives, and actions. This is a vitally important reason why they should be embraced as an important part of accountability.

Other obstacles exist. Alternative assessments are new; it takes time and energy to re-educate teachers, parents, and students in new forms of assessments. Moreover, such assessments cost more because they require more sophisticated teaching, staff development, and scoring.

Nor are alternative assessments a magic bullet. Teachers and parents need to be aware of the strengths and weaknesses of any approach, and how to use it appropriately.

Following is a description of some of the most common forms of alternative assessments that can replace traditional tests.

Portfolio-Based Assessment

One of the more promising forms of assessment is what is known as "portfolio-based assessment." The approaches to portfolios vary considerably, but they all rest on records kept by the teacher and on collections of the student's work, called the "student portfolio." During the school year, teachers and students gather work which shows student progress and achievement in various subjects such as English or science. Students are usually encouraged to reflect on the work that has been selected. Such reflection helps students think not only about what they have learned, but about their own learning processes, all of which contributes to the overall goal of improving student learning.

In some approaches, at the end of a marking period the teacher examines the portfolio and evaluates the work based on a scoring guide. Sometimes students or their peers also score their work. The teacher ultimately records a score on what is sometimes called a "learning record," attaching evidence such as a writing sample or write-up of a science experiment. This approach is useful for the teacher and parent in determining how well a student is progressing. But, through what is known as "random sampling," it also can be the basis for improved professional development and for school- and district-wide accountability.

Under "random sampling," a number of the learning records and student portfolios are selected randomly from each classroom. An independent group — of teachers from other schools, members of the community, or a combination of both — reviews the records and portfolios. If there is a big difference between the conclusions of the independent readers and the classroom teacher, a third group might be called in or a larger sample might be taken from the classroom, in order to determine how well a particular teacher consistently applies the agreed upon assessment guidelines.

Approaches of this sort have been developed

in Britain, Australia, and the United States, particularly in Vermont, which has instituted statewide assessment programs in math and writing based on student portfolios. Projects such as the Learning Record, based in California, and the Work Sampling System, based in Ann Arbor, are other examples. (see Resources p. 139)

This classroom-based approach has several advantages. For example, the evaluation is based on a wide range of student work done over a long period of time, rather than on a single, paper-and-pencil test taken over a few hours. Further, the approach encourages schools and districts to invest in the professional development of the teachers and outside evaluators, and it pushes teachers to reflect more consistently on the quality of student work in their classroom.

One criticism of the portfolio approach is that it relies too much on the individual judgment of teachers and opens the door to overly subjective evaluation. This concern has been raised most directly where teachers may not be sensitive to the needs and skills of students of color, or non-English speakers, or immigrants. Clearly, this is a serious issue. At the same time, it is a problem that pervades all forms of assessment. Who, for example, chooses the questions on standardized tests? Rarely is it immigrants, or non-English speakers, or educators of color.

Adopting alternatives isn't easy. Old ways of doing things are always more comfortable and familiar.

If the outside evaluators are sensitive to this potential problem, portfolio-based assessment can be used to identify teachers who are subjectively giving lower evaluations to particular groups of students or teachers whose pedagogical weaknesses lead them to have students focus on mindless worksheets rather than engaging projects.

Performance Exams

Some states and districts have adopted what are called performance examinations. These are tests given to all students, based on students "performing" a certain task, such as writing an essay, conducting a science experiment, or doing an oral presentation which is videotaped.

The Milwaukee Public Schools have done extensive work on developing such performance exams in the areas of writing, science, math, visual arts, and oral communications. For example, fourth or fifth graders must perform a 3-5 minute oral presentation. In writing, fourth, fifth, eighth, 11th, and 12th graders all have to write and revise an essay over a period of two days, based on a district-wide prompt that changes from year to year and covers different genres, from imaginary writing, to narrative essays, to expository essays. These essays are then judged independently and anonymously by teachers from the district, using a scale of one to four. Two teachers read each essay, and the final score is based on the sum of the two readers. To reduce subjectivity, if there is a difference of more than one point in the two readers' evaluation, a third reader scores the paper.

Some districts also use these performance exams as a way to check how well classroom teachers are scoring their student portfolios. If large numbers of students are doing well on the performance exams yet score poorly on the student portfolios, or vice versa, it sends a signal that follow-up needs to occur.

These performance exams have the advantage over standardized tests in that they "drive the curriculum" in a relatively progressive way. In Milwaukee, the assessments have encouraged teachers to focus on actual student writing rather than fill-in-the-blank work sheets. They have led to more hands-on science experiments where students actually learn the scientific process and how to reflect on and analyze data, rather than merely answer questions at the end of a textbook chapter. The oral presentations have been a useful way to get students actively involved, rather than merely listening to lectures by the teacher; they also force teachers to pay attention to oral communication skills, which cannot be tested with a paper-and-pencil exam. The actual performance assessments, once they are scored, can become part of student portfolios.

Teachers who help write the performance assessment tasks (or prompts) learn a lot about how to develop more interesting and academically valuable projects for their students.

Performance exams are one form of "performance assessments" which most often take the form of projects, from laboratory experiments to group activities to exhibitions (described below) which are done as part of classroom work. (Sometimes the term includes portfolios as well.) Using performance exams can encourage teachers to use a wider range of activities in the classroom, which can enrich instruction, deepen learning, and provide detailed assessment information.

Performance exams have not been used more widely in part because they take considerable time, both for the classroom teacher and the district. It takes time, expertise, and ultimately money to develop the prompts and score the assessments, to say nothing of training teachers in activity-based teaching methods necessary for such performance assessments.

As with using random sampling of student portfolios, sampling can also be used with performance exams. The National Assessment of Educational Progress (NAEP), a federal agency that monitors student achievement, uses such a sampling technique. When the NAEP reports, for example, on the progress of U.S. fourth graders, the data is based on a sample of students. (The NAEP exam uses multiple-choice and somewhat longer written responses).

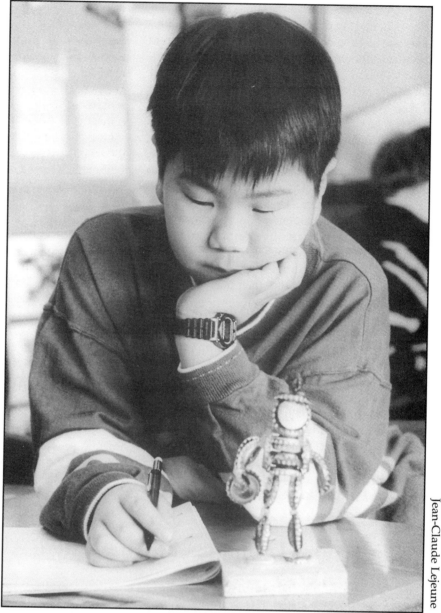

Jean-Claude Lejeune

Exit Standards

The assessment known as "proficiency exit standards" combines the approaches of portfolio-based assessment and performance exams; it also sometimes includes standardized tests.

Under this approach, students have to meet certain standards in order to be promoted to the next grade or to graduate from high school. In Milwaukee, for example, the district has developed proficiencies that students need to meet in order to complete eighth grade and graduate from high school. The proficiency standards focus on four broad areas — math, science, communication, and a research project— and are generally considered more rigorous than most standardized exams.

Students are given several ways to show "proficiency" in each of these areas — through portfolios, classroom projects such as science projects, performance exams, standardized test scores, and research papers. Students may do poorly on one assessment method but show proficiency through other methods.

Exhibitions

Exhibitions of student work are another useful assessment. Perhaps the most common exhibition is also one of the oldest — the science fair. As with any student work, the strength of the approach rests on providing ways for all students to succeed. Everyone knows stories of parents who do the science fair project for their kid, building elaborate electrical engines or wondrous weather kits. Some schools try to get around this problem by having students work on the projects at school.

At Central Park East in New York City, exhibitions are used along with portfolios. In order to graduate, students have to demonstrate competencies in 12 areas of learning and present their portfolio work to a committee of adults — somewhat similar to the oral exams common for postgraduate degrees.

At La Escuela Fratney in Milwaukee, at the end of fifth grade (before they leave for middle school), students select some of their work from throughout the year and invite family and community members to an open exhibition. One project that figures prominently is the student-made book, in which students reflect on what they've learned throughout elementary school. The book also includes examples of work from their entire time at Fratney, which have been collected as part of their portfolios.

Parent Conferences and Input

One important reason for assessment is to let parents know how well their child is progressing. This purpose cannot be separated from the larger issue of communication between school and home. A number of schools are experimenting with assessment programs that are based on a process of two-way communication.

Some schools, for instance, have lengthy conferences with parents before their child even enters kindergarten, both explaining the schools' programs and getting input from the family on the child's strengths and weaknesses. Other schools have adapted their parent-teacher conferences so that they do a better job of letting parents and teachers talk together about the child's progress. In order for such an approach to work, parent-teacher conferences need to go beyond the "five minutes per teacher" syndrome that is particularly common in middle and high schools — where teachers haul out the grade book and talk, and parents listen.

In this approach, schools need to ensure that they give parents a clear idea of the school's curriculum and a general view of child development. This is particularly important in early elementary grades, where children develop at different rates and ages and children cannot be pigeon-holed into a single set of expectations. Likewise, in adolescence, teachers and parents need to communicate about developmental issues and how they may be affecting student performance.

Some schools involve students in the conferences. Students are asked to present work from their portfolios, reflect on what they have learned, and help figure out where they have made good progress and where they still need work.

To work best, such an approach needs to be part of a comprehensive effort to ensure that parents know they can raise concerns at any point during the school year, not just at conference time. Soliciting and encouraging such parental input is not easy but is essential if there is to be a true collaboration between home and school.

Classroom Examples of Alternative Assessment

How can teachers motivate students to produce quality work?

Fifth-grade teacher Bob Peterson explains some of the ways in which he tries to inspire his students with activities ranging from student work porfolios, to student reflections, to student projects, to student-led parent/teacher conferences. The efforts culminate in an end-of-the-year exhibition of student work for parents and community.

For the full text of his article, "Motivating Students to Do Quality Work," go to www.rethinkingschools.org, under "Past Issues," Vol. 12, #2, Spring 1998.

✳   ✳   ✳

High school teacher Linda Christensen has extensively used portfolios to encourage students to reflect upon and improve their work. In an article that appeared in Rethinking Schools, Christensen explains in detail how she helps the students develop their portfolios — from providing sufficient time for quality work, to giving them models and prompts for reflection. She also reflects on what she has learned as a teacher and what needs to be done to improve the portfolio process.

For the full text of her article, "Basketball and Portfolios: A Classroom Look at Authentic Assessment," go to www.rethinkingschools.org, under "Past Issues," Vol. 9, #3, in the Spring .

School Report Cards

Just as parents need to know how well their child is doing, communities have the right to know how well entire schools are performing. Sometimes, this happens in a rather distorted way: the local newspaper ranks schools based on a single standardized test or battery of tests. Beyond the cold hard number, there is little analysis of how or why some schools are performing differently — or even if the test is a valid measure of student achievement. Equally troubling, a school's performance often tells more about the income level of the students' families than the quality of teaching and learning at the school.

In the last few years, a growing number of schools have issued "school report cards" — in fact, over two-thirds of states now require such report cards, and many are posted on web sites.

School report cards generally go beyond a listing of test scores, although that data is included. Other information in the report, depending on the state or district, can include attendance, average grade point, the number of Advanced Placement courses, discipline issues such as suspension rates, parental involvement, types of assessment (such as whether performance exams are required in certain subjects) and their results, school mission and governance structure, and so forth. The information is sometimes broken down by race, gender, socio-economic status, first language, and other important categories, in order to show how well schools are serving students from diverse backgrounds.

While such report cards are superior to a simple listing of test scores, there are important cautions: in particular, data can be omitted or manipulated. Some high schools, for example, have a policy of dropping students from a class if they have more than three unexcused absences. As a result, the grade point average in that class can be artificially high because only a select group of students is included. Also, if the primary data on student learning is from standardized test scores, as is often the case, then parents will have too little information about important areas of learning.

School Quality Review Teams

Because student success is intimately related to the culture of learning in an entire school, one valuable assessment, known as the "School Quality Review Team," focuses on school-wide issues.

Teams of trained educators and community members visit schools, usually for up to a week. The teams observe classrooms, follow students, examine the curriculum, and interview parents and teachers. Based on their observations, they write up a formal report, with specific recommendations for improvement.

This approach, modeled on a century-old system in England, has been adopted in a few states, including New York and Rhode Island. A growing number of schools in Boston use review teams.

To be most effective, the team's recommendations need to be distributed to and acted upon by both teachers and parents — which often requires additional time and resources. Another shortcoming in this approach is that the team often reviews a school based on its self-described mission; if the mission is weak or inadequate, this might not be noted in the final report.

It Won't Be Easy

Adopting these alternatives isn't easy — old ways of doing things are always more comfortable and familiar. Here are some of the most common pitfalls:

■ Most alternatives take time to develop. Because most are implemented while existing standardized tests continue, teachers are being asked to do more and more assessing — but not given any more time to do so.

■ If such assessments are to provide a true alternative, it's essential that a broad array of parents and staff be involved.

■ Many of these alternative assessments are new to just about everyone involved: policy-makers, students, teachers, and parents. There needs to be thorough discussions of the pros and cons of various assessments, and clear understanding of the purpose of any particular assessment.

■ Such assessments take more work, more time, and more resources.

■ Any assessment is prone to problems of inequity, inadequacy, and subjectivity. Recognizing, and counteracting, these problems is essential.

Finally, it cannot be stated too often: the primary purpose of assessment is to improve the quality of teaching and to help students learn better. If the focus is not on student learning, it's misplaced. ❐

— Bob Peterson (repmilw@aol.com) teaches in Milwaukee and is an editor of Rethinking Schools. Monty Neill (Mneillft@aol.com) is Executive Director of FairTest, based in Cambridge, MA.

The above article is excerpted from a longer analysis that appeared in Rethinking Schools, Vol. 13, #3, Spring 1999. The full text can be found at www.rethinkingschools.org under "Past Issues."

What Is the Purpose Of Assessment?

If the goal is making sure children are learning properly, standardized tests are not the best way to get there.

BY MONTY NEILL

The controversies over standards and testing have at times encouraged unhealthy views on the purposes of assessment: as status markers for status-conscious parents, means to punish or bribe teachers, mechanisms to sort students by race and class.

But the primary purpose of assessment should be to improve student learning.

This basic idea underlies "Principles and Indicators for Student Assessment Systems," a report released by the National Forum on Assessment, a national coalition of education and civil rights groups. Building on exemplary practice around the country, the report proposes that the traditional, test-driven approach to measuring student achievement be replaced by assessment which is:

- Fair to all students.
- Strengthened by professional collaboration and development.
- Developed and monitored with broad community involvement.
- Supported by systematic and clear communication.
- Regularly reviewed and improved.

Classroom Assessment

In the Forum's model, assessment becomes a set of rich, varied, classroom practices, focusing on observation, documentation, and evaluation of actual student work done over time. Interwoven with curriculum and instruction, it requires teachers to give students:

- Multiple ways to demonstrate learning;
- Active learning opportunities through projects, exhibitions, performances, and portfolios, as well as exams;
- Choice and self-evaluation; and
- Individual as well as group work.

> **The primary purpose of assessment should be to improve student learning.**

The Primary Language Record or its California adaptation, the Learning Record, provides one model for the assessment of elementary school children. The Language Record is a process and tool used to assess how well a child is learning to read and write. At the start of the year, the teacher interviews each student and her/his parent(s) and summarizes the interviews on recording forms. In the interviews, the teacher talks with parents and students about how the child learns, about her or his reading/writing behavior and interests. Teachers and parents alike have found this process to be a powerful way to break down school-parent barriers and to help teachers best understand their students.

In using this model, a teacher keeps track of student work through observation and documentation, collecting the products of work and taking notes on things the student does and says. The teacher relies on a blend of detailed observations, interviews, and discussions. Occasionally, the teacher might quiz or test the students to check on their understanding or their ability to do something. Several times a year, the teacher pulls together all the information and prepares summaries of each student's learning. The LR provides a structure for this summary evaluation. In higher grades, the student work documented can grow to include computer-based work, essays, lab experiments, and performance exams. The summaries, together with work samples, provide a rich portrait of a student to be shared with the student, parents, and other teachers.

Strengthening Equity

This approach encourages teachers to have regular discussions in order to review student work, strengthen their knowledge of students, confront their own biases, and learn how to improve their teaching. Assessment then can help teachers work as a community of learners, able to collaborate on the difficult task of confronting their own biases. The documentation produced can also help provide accountability to the community. For example, if Latino children in a particular school or district generally do not perform as well as White/Anglo children on samples of portfolios or on exams given on a sampling basis, an investigative team could look in more detail at the portfolios, work samples, etc. from the classroom in order to determine the cause of the gap and take action. School practice can thus be held up to scrutiny, as has been done with portfolios in Pittsburgh.

There are important practical conclusions that flow from the Principles. For example, the National Forum on Assessment believes that decisions about students, such as high school graduation or grade promotion, should not be made on the basis of any single assessment. Decisions should be based on information about student work and accomplishments collected over time. This is, of course, how it has been done for most of our nation's history. It can be done better by using the tools of performance assessment and evaluation.

Accountability is often the reason given for imposing standardized tests. However, accountability data can come from evidence of student learning in their classrooms, such as samples of portfolios. Performance-based exams, administered on a sampling basis, can be used to complement the classroom information. Through these approaches, the public will have more and richer information about real learning, and students and teachers will be freed from the harmful burden of standardized, multiple-choice tests.

Transforming Assessment

To make such changes possible, schools must be restructured to allow teachers and other educators time to work with each other in restructuring curriculum, instruction and assessment, and in developing schools as communities of active learners. The wider community, too, and especially parents, must be part of the broad planning to reshape assessment along with other aspects of schooling. Parent and community groups, as well as civil rights organizations and other concerned

Marilyn Nolt

people, will have to actively insist on positive changes in the system.

Assessments substantially define not only what we expect our children to learn, but also how we think they learn and the kinds of learning environments that will be constructed to support that learning. The Principles call for equity and diversity, stimulating and supportive learning environments, high standards, critical thinking, and the fuller development of the individual and the community. They stand against a narrow conception of learning and knowledge that has, for the sake of efficiency and social sorting, too long dominated schooling.

Implementing the Principles certainly cannot alone overcome the many problems facing schools, but they speak to what can be accomplished by assessment as part of broader school reform. ❐

— *Monty Neill is co-chair of the National Forum on Assessment and Executive Director of the National Center for Fair & Open Testing (FairTest).The Principles can be ordered from FairTest, 342 Broadway, Cambridge, MA 02139. 617-864-4810. fairtest@fairtest.org for $10.00, which includes s&h. Call for bulk discount prices. An order form is available at www.fairtest.org. The Learning Record can be found at www.learningrecord.org/ or 10610 Quail Canyon Rd., El Cajon, CA 92021.*

The above is excerpted from an article that was printed in Rethinking Schools, Vol. 10, #4, Summer 1996. The full version is available online at www.rethinkingschools.org under "Past Issues."

Alternative Assessment

A community-based group in Massachusetts outlines an accountability program that is not based on standardized tests.

The Coalition for Authentic reform in Education (CARE) in Massachusetts is mounting a campaign for an assessment program that does not undermine effective classroom practices. CARE is proposing a four-part plan that includes: local authentic assessments, a school quality review process, limited standardized testing in literacy and math, and annual school reports to communities. For a complete copy of the CARE proposal go to www.fairtest.org or contact CARE (see Resources p. 141). Excerpts from the CARE proposal follow.

■ Local authentic assessments that are gateways to graduation, approved by regional boards and based on the Common Core of Learning [a short statement of essential learning goals rather than the overly detailed curriculum Framework of Standards].

CARE supports an assessment system in which districts and schools, rather than the state, would determine graduation. CARE supports having the state define an essential, but limited, body of knowledge, skills, and habits of mind that all students should acquire.

In this case, the [state's] Curriculum Frameworks become a guide, rather than a required body of knowledge to master.

Using the [state's] Common Core and a streamlined set of competencies, each school in the Commonwealth would develop its own accountability and assessment plan. The plan, developed by teachers, administrators, and parents, and approved by the school council and district, would outline how the school will ensure that students demonstrate that they meet the Common Core.

Each school would submit its accountability plan to a regional board, established by the Massachusetts Department of Education, which would include teachers, administrators, parents, higher education representatives, business representatives, community people, students, and state education agency staff.

■ A school quality review model to assess the effectiveness of school practices, based on the successful models in Britain, Boston's Pilot Schools, Rhode Island, and Massachusetts' own model for charter schools.

In addition to assessing what students know and are able to do, a genuine accountability system also assesses the quality of opportunities, resources, instruction, and curriculum that are offered to students. A key goal of school quality reviews is to ensure equitable and quality resources and learning opportunities are being provided to all students, and that the school can demonstrate it is working to improve achievement of all students while also closing the achievement gap between low-income and affluent students, and between white students and students of color.

In a school quality review process, all schools would be placed on a three- to five-year cycle for review and evaluation. The state would develop a set of benchmarks for successful schools. A school selected for review would engage in self-study to assess where it stood in reaching the benchmarks, and collect evidence in the form of a school portfolio to demonstrate its progress in meeting them.

The state would then send in a team, made up of school practitioners from other districts and other qualified people, to spend an intensive 3-4 days to observe students and teachers, interview parents, review the portfolio, and collect evidence to determine whether progress toward meeting the benchmarks was being made. In particular, the team would also review a random sampling of

> **CARE supports an assessment system in which districts and schools, rather than the state, would determine graduation.**

assessments of students who have graduated or been promoted, to determine whether the school's assessments and the students' performances meet the demands of the Common Core and state benchmarks.

Schools failing to reach the benchmarks would be placed on a one-year follow-up review cycle, with further intervention required if the school still did not make progress. CARE agrees that schools which fail to serve their students well and which are unable to improve despite help should not be allowed to continue without significant intervention.

■ Standardized testing solely in literacy and numeracy, to provide one method for tracking progress of schools from year to year.

The state may still feel the need to have data that can be compared to other states, and across districts. In this case, while recognizing their limitations, inherent biases, and potential danger to instruction and curriculum, CARE supports the limited use of standardized testing as an additional source of information. Such tests should not have high stakes attached to them, should take only a few hours to administer, and should assess only literacy and numeracy. CARE also believes parents should have the right to opt their children out of standardized testing.

■ Required annual local reporting by schools to their communities, using a defined set of indicators, which also focus on equal opportunity and access to knowledge for all students.

Genuine accountability also requires public reporting to the community. However, this reporting has much more meaning when it is locally tailored to the needs of the community. In this case, CARE advocates that the state develop a list of indicators that every school and district must annually report to their respective communities. This list of indicators should include reporting on outcomes of students by race, gender, low-income status, special needs, and limited English proficiency. Schools and districts would be required to disseminate their reports to parents and the community, while also sending them to the Massachusetts Department of Education.

In this public, decentralized system of genuine accountability, the state education agency assumes a resource and monitoring role. It provides technical assistance with portfolio development, appropriate uses of tests, the development of performance tasks, examples of organizing public exhibitions, uses of rubrics, and protocols for public reporting. The state annual report would include local examples of authentic assessments, as well as aggregate data on student performance. The state's role, then, also becomes one of disseminating and promoting best instructional, curriculum, and assessment practices.

While preserving a focus on high standards for all students and public accountability for all schools, this system of genuine accountability also encourages and promotes local innovation, creativity, and freedom. ❑

A Racial Justice Report Card

An Oakland-area advocacy group has issued a computer-based program which produces a "Racial Justice Report Card" for a school or school district. The program is particularly geared toward parent and community groups who want to evaluate how well students of color are doing within the schools.

The program outlines a series of steps to compile information on a range of topics: drop-out, graduation, and college attendance rates; discipline practices; access to equal resources and facilities; multicultural curricula composition of the teaching staff, and others. The program suggests how to get such information, how to organize the data, and how to publicize findings and propose solutions. While the program does not cover all areas — for example it does not address tracking, disparities in grade point averages, or the quality of staff training on multicultural/anti-racist issues — it offers a highly user-friendly way for parents and community organizers to investigate racial discrimination in the schools.

"Making the Grade" is produced by ERASE (Expose Racism and Advance School Excellence), a project of the Applied Research Center of Oakland, CA. For more information about ERASE, visit the ARC website - www.arc.org. The program can be ordered through Chardon Press at 1-888-458-8588.

Their Report Card — and Ours

*Portland area teachers develop a school report card
that does not rely on standardized tests.*

The Oregon Department of Education recently began issuing "report cards" which judge a school almost exclusively on the basis of standardized tests. Members of Portland Area Rethinking Schools (PARS) believe that this will turn schools into "test prep academies" that drill around a narrow range of skills — in the process stifling academic rigor and love of learning.

In response, PARS members drafted an alternative "report card" that emphasizes school attributes which encourage young people to become enthusiastic and sophisticated learners.

The PARS teachers emphasize that the process of designing and collecting data for such a report card is just as important as the product which emerges. PARS asserts that "real school reform must be democratic, drawing on the collective efforts of teachers, students, administrators, parents, and the broader community."

Assessment that is developed from the school community can be a way to look thoughtfully at school practices, with a keen eye toward finding practical ways to remedy long-standing problems.

Following are excerpts from the PARS report card. The report card is offered not as a blueprint for wholesale adoption, but as an example of how concerned educators and community members can work together to set up and implement a meaningful system of accountability.

A complete copy of the PARS Report Card is available at www.rethinkingschools.org, under the special section on standards and testing.

What power does the community have in decision–making?

Curriculum

■ How is the content of the curriculum meaningful, interdisciplinary, multicultural, and academically rigorous for all students?

■ How are high academic expectations communicated to and maintained for all students?

■ How are historic, artistic, and scientific contributions of diverse cultures, families, social classes, and genders represented in each content area?

■ How does the curriculum encourage all students to see themselves as social and environmental problem-solvers capable of making the world a better place? Does the curriculum have real life links?

■ Are there sufficient resources available to meet the curricular mission of the school? For example:

— What is the range of actual class sizes?

— Do students have access to mentors and tutors?

— Are reading, writing, math, and/or other specialists available for students and staff?

— What school time is scheduled for teachers to plan, develop, and discuss curriculum?

Student Assessment

■ How is it ensured that assessment allows students multiple ways to demonstrate their learning?

■ How is it ensured that the frequent use of feedback from assessments offers students the opportunity to grow?

■ How do assessment results influence subsequent instruction in the classroom and program modification in the school?

■ What actions are taken to avoid misapplication of assessment results through tracking or stigmatization?

Equity for All Students

■ Historically, so-called ability grouping has discriminated against poor and working class students and students of color by offering educational programs of unequal quality to different students. How does the school group its students (e.g., honors, advanced, remedial, scholars, International Baccalaureate)? How does the school know any policies or practices that hinder efforts to provide all students with quality education?

■ What accommodations are made for the needs of students with attendance and tardy problems: students who work to support their families, travel to home countries, take care of younger or older family members?

■ Is there evidence of historical, literary, artistic, and scientific contributions of diverse cultures represented in each content area? in teachers' lesson plans? in the bookroom? on bulletin boards? during assemblies?

■ Who is represented and honored in the school? Consider the hallways, library, and overall school environment. Does the racial, ethnic, linguistic, and class composition of extra-curricular leadership and special academic programs reflect the student body? How are low-income, minority, or second language students encouraged to participate?

Health and Safety

■ Describe your discipline policies and programs that promote respect and conflict intervention and resolution. Specifically, how are students involved in these programs?

■ How does the school promote the physical safety and the emotional well-being of students? Are programs built into the curriculum addressing such needs as violence and sexual harassment prevention, suicide intervention, sex education, and prevention of drug and alcohol abuse?

■ How are marginalized students identified and protected at your school? What policies and strategies are used to counter racist, sexist or homophobic language and put-downs? How is respect taught in the school curriculum?

■ How accessible are mental health and crisis services at the school? Is nursing staff provided? Describe safe places students can go during personal distress. Describe any formal or informal mental health services available to students.

■ What is the selection and quality of cafeteria food? Are restricted or organic diets available? What are the school policies about serving milk and meat products from hormone-injected animals or other genetically-modified foods? How often and under what criteria is the water tested in the school?

■ How is the student environment protected from other chemical ingredients of unknown or potentially harmful effects — e.g., in cleaning solutions, herbicides, pesticides, or airborne contaminants?

Parents and Community in the Life of the School

■ How does the school include parents, students, and community in decision making?

■ What adaptation and/or encouragement is made for working, non-English speaking, marginalized parents and/or parents of color?

■ What power does the community have in decision–making?

■ When and how are parents informed and included regarding student progress (e.g., academic assessments, absences, tardiness, and misconduct)?

■ How does school ensure parents understand their student's progress?

■ Is there broad representation of community organizations in the life of the school: unions, women's organizations, religious institutions, senior centers, environmental and social justice organizations, businesses, etc.?

■ How is school networked to other community services? How does the school facilitate connecting students and families to community and governmental resources?

■ How does the school reach out to the community during transition points — i.e., from preschool into kindergarten or first grade? from elementary to middle school? from middle school to high school? from high school to college?

■ In the school, how are parents and/or community members invited to give feedback on student work or portfolios? Are there student author presentations, science fairs, gallery displays, etc.?

■ What informational events does the school hold?

District and State Support

■ In what ways do the school district and state support the school community in achieving the above aims?

■ In what ways do the school district and state hinder the school community in achieving the above aims?

■ What strategies are being pursued by the school community to challenge any policies or practices that hinder efforts to provide all students with quality education? ❐

For more information e-mail: BBPDX@aol.com

Portland Area Rethinking Schools shares the mission and goals of Rethinking Schools, but operates independently of the Rethinking Schools Editorial Board.

Alternatives to Grade Retention

'No social promotion!' is the latest sound-bite reform. But if the goal is to improve classroom learning, other strategies make more sense.

BY LINDA DARLING-HAMMOND

When policymakers urge that students be held accountable for low achievement, they frequently call for grade retention and the withholding of diplomas. The assumption is that consequences will motivate children to achieve, and if they do not, the low-performing students should just keep repeating the material until they get it right.

Yet dozens of studies have found that retaining students actually contributes to greater academic failure, higher levels of dropping out, and greater behavioral difficulties. Students who are held back actually do worse in the long run than comparable students who are promoted, in part perhaps because they do not receive better or more appropriate teaching when they are retained, and in part because they give up on themselves as learners.

New York City's Promotional Gates Program, ultimately discontinued in the late 1980s, resulted in 12-year-olds stuck in the 4th grade and 17-year-olds sitting in 8th-grade classrooms.

Even small children perceive that being held back is a stigma. One study found that children fear grade retention so much that they cite it third on their list of anxieties, following only the fear of blindness and death of a parent.

Shifting Blame

The premise of grade retention as a solution for poor performance is that the problem, if there is one, resides in the child rather than in the schooling he or she has encountered. Instead of looking carefully at classroom or school practices, schools typically send students back to repeat the same experience. Little is done to ensure that the experience will be either more appropriate for the individual child or of higher quality. This is particularly troubling given mounting evidence that children's unequal access to high-quality curriculum and teaching is strongly related to their achievement.

Not only have recent studies found that teacher expertise is by far the single most important determinant of student performance, but low-income, minority, and special-needs students are least likely to receive well-qualified, highly effective teachers. Tracking systems often heighten these effects by assigning the least-qualified teachers to the lowest-achieving students year after year.

However, the negative effects of grade retention should not become an argument for social promotion — that is, the practice of moving students through the system without ensuring they acquire the skills they need. If neither retention nor social promotion is effective, what are the alternatives?

There are at least four complementary strategies school administrators can employ:

■ Enhancing professional development for teachers to ensure that they have the knowledge and skills they need to teach a wider range of students to meet the standards;

■ Redesigning school structures to support more intensive learning;

■ Ensuring that targeted supports and services are available for students when they are needed; and

■ Employing classroom assessments that better inform teaching.

> *Children fear grade retention so much that they cite it third on their list of anxieties, following only fear of blindness and death of a parent.*

Jean-Claude Lejeune

Skillful Teaching

Highly skilled teachers who know how to use a wide range of successful teaching strategies adapted to diverse learners are, of course, the most important alternative to grade retention. Teaching that is developmentally, cognitively, and culturally responsive enables a greater range of students to succeed.

As discussed in the National Commission on Teacher's latest report "Doing What Matters Most," teacher expertise has been found to be the most significant determinant of student success, accounting for as much as 40% of the difference in overall student performance. Students who have highly effective teachers three years in a row score as much as 50 percentile points higher on achievement tests than those who have ineffective teachers for three years in a row. Several studies have found that the disparities in achievement between Black and White students are largely a function of differences in the qualifications of the teachers they are assigned.

NO COMMENT

All those who are getting mediocre scores on your SATs, take heart. You, too, might be a presidential candidate. George W. Bush received an SAT verbal score of 566.

Unfortunately, many veteran teachers were not trained to meet many of today's expectations for the teaching of reading, mathematics, and other subjects. They have no preparation for teaching students with learning disabilities or those whose first language is not English. They were not taught about how people learn or how to support learning of different kinds.

While newly prepared teachers often have had more access to this knowledge, many new teachers are hired who have had little or no teacher training. In 1994, nearly 25% of newly hired teachers lacked full preparation for their jobs. The proportions were higher in many urban and poor rural schools with large concentrations of low-income and minority students. Neither standards nor assessments can help students achieve if they do not have competent teachers to support them in their learning.

Redesigning Schools

Teaching strategies that address differences in how students learn while aiming for common high standards often require organizational changes that provide more extended contact between teachers and students.

When age grading was adopted from the Prussian educational system nearly a century ago, it seemed an efficient way to structure teachers' work, to apply sequential curriculum guides, and to move students through a more tightly specified system. However, as it was implemented, the practice of age grading had two negative side effects:

■ It reduced the time individual teachers spent with groups of students and hence their ability to come to know those students well; and

■ It reduced the opportunities for older, more competent peers to help socialize and assist their younger colleagues, thus removing a potent teaching resource from the classroom.

Recent research has found that students experience much greater success in schools structured to create close, sustained relationships among students and teachers. In high-achieving countries like Japan, Germany, Sweden, and Switzerland, teachers often stay with the same students for two or more years and teach them more than one subject.

Targeted Services

Census Bureau data show that in 1995, more

> *Teacher expertise is by far the single most important determinant of student performance.*

than a third of children with learning disabilities had repeated at least one grade in school. However, research suggests that most were not helped and many were harmed by this solution to their problems. While there is a growing consensus that the last decade's approaches to the provision of special education and other categorical services have become problematic, appropriately targeted services are still needed for many students.

Serious efforts are needed to correct the flawed identification practices, fragmented and ineffective service delivery models, and undertraining of personnel that leave many special-needs children in low-quality settings with watered-down curriculum.

However, there are circumstances in which individual students have special learning needs that are not well-addressed in regular classroom settings. For every horror story about inappropriate placement and teaching, there are success stories about students who were helped to learn by special services that were well targeted to their specific learning needs and delivered by well-prepared teachers with the necessary skills.

For the estimated 10-20% of students who have visual/perceptual disabilities similar to dyslexia, for example, such specific assistance is essential to success throughout the school career. In addition, most students who are identified as failing in the early grades are struggling in the

NO COMMENT

Mount Holyoke Drops SAT Requirement

Mount Holyoke, the country's oldest college for women, has decided that it will no longer require that students submit SAT and ACT scores as part of the admissions process.

The college, based in South Hadley, MA, took the step after the faculty endorsed the test-score optional policy, after a committee report concluded that "the SAT scores, at best, are a measure of a narrow set of verbal and mathematical abilities. The test does not measure the range of intellectual and emotional qualities that our own educational environment requires and attempts to nourish."

area of literacy development, which is a key to school success from the first years on.

Students who are falling behind can be helped by extra time routinely provided each day after school (some schools build extra-help periods into teachers' and students' schedules), by resource room teachers and trained student or adult tutors, and by Saturday school or summer school.

The key is that these opportunities — unlike most uses of summer school, Saturday school or resource rooms — must be readily and routinely available to all students as soon as they need help. They must also be linked directly to the current work they are doing in the classroom, and must offer them help from individuals who understand both the content and skills the teacher is trying to pursue and the nature of the difficulty the student is experiencing.

Skjold Photographs

Useful Assessments

Ensuring that students get the specific help they need requires rich information about what they know and can do, as well as how they learn. Assessments that give detailed information about students' approaches to learning as well as about their levels of performance can determine how students can be helped most successfully, rather than merely whether they will be held back or passed on.

Unfortunately, standardized tests that rely on multiple-choice formats give little information about the learning process or students' abilities to produce analyses or products. Consequently, many educators are developing assessments that engage students in performance tasks that reflect standards in a given field, such as essay examinations, oral presentations, problem-solving exercises, research projects, and collections of work, as well as systematic teacher observations.

Many educators who use these kinds of performance assessments confirm that such assessments provide information about how students think, what they understand, and the strategies they use in their learning.

The diagnostic teaching that this enables future teachers to undertake is the strongest argument for new standards and assessments: the creation of a system that is attentive to what students have learned and is responsive to their learning needs. That would constitute genuine accountability. ❐

— Linda Darling-Hammond is a professor of teaching and teacher education at Stanford University. This article is condensed from an article in the August 1998 issue of The School Administrator.

Assumptions Behind Assessments

BY MARY DIEZ

Following are some of the often unspoken assumptions behind different types of assessment. The assessments are broken down into two main categories: assessments that are part of the teacher's curriculum and teaching; and standardized assessments, both multiple choice formats and performance assessments, that are given under standardized conditions.

Looking at the assumptions highlights some of the differences in the types of assessments. For example, curriculum-based assessments tend to be focused on providing information, over time, that will improve student learning. Standardized assessments tend to be one-time evaluations focused on comparing students and schools.

— Mary Diez is graduate dean at Alverno College in Milwaukee, WI. The following is adapted from her forthcoming work, "Assessing Student Competence in Teacher Education Programs," in Assessment of Student Competence in Accredited Disciplines, T. Banta & C. Palomba eds., (Stylus Publishing.)

Curriculum-based Assessment

■ A wide range of curriculum standards can be addressed, both because there is time to do so and because multiple modes of assessment can be used over time.

■ Conditions may vary; assessments take place in the classroom context.

■ Prompts and modes can be designed locally or drawn upon a central bank of samples; while guidelines should be used in the design and development, staff continuously develop assessments to meet the needs of students and refine them as they learn from their use.

■ Assessments look more like assignments and are not separate from good assignments.

■ Assessments can take place over time and can be revised; students build a track record of performance and can keep it in a portfolio.

■ The assessment process is cumulative, with the body of work developing an ever-richer picture of the student's performance.

■ Faculty who work with students develop a community of professional judgment through which they share understanding and apply criteria. This community of professional judgment is the source of reliability of judgment.

■ Feedback is a central means of improving student performance and self assessment is a critical process for student learning.

Standardized Testing

■ Aspects of the curriculum standards are selected, based both upon what is judged to be important and what can be measured most effectively.

■ Assessments take place under prescribed conditions.

■ Prompts and modes of responses are standardized, having been developed through a rigorous process of development, pilot testing, and field testing.

■ Prompts and modes need to be "secure."

■ The assessment is a one-time event.

■ The assessment is "summative," with a cut score.

■ Cut scores are determined through a process for which assessors are trained to meet a standard of judgment; reliability is a process of meeting a psychometric standard.

■ Little or no feedback is given to the student.

FAILING OUR KIDS:
WHY THE TESTING CRAZE WON'T FIX OUR SCHOOLS

Jean-Claude Lejeune

Policy
And
Background

Testing: Full Speed Ahead

Governors and CEOs met at the National Education Summit to press their system of standards, high-stakes tests, and 'rewards and consequences.'

BY
BARBARA MINER

PALISADES, NY — President Clinton, 24 governors, 33 business leaders, 19 state superintendents and education commissioners, and 35 invited guests gathered at the National Education Summit at IBM headquarters in early October 1999 to discuss standards and plot the next stage in the reform of U.S. schools.

In an improvement over previous summits, representatives of education organizations were invited, ranging from the teacher's unions to the National Association of State School Boards. But no principals or teachers were allowed in, no students participated, and the only representative of a non-white advocacy organization was Hugh Price of the National Urban League.

After a day-and-a-half of discussion, conference participants dispersed, by and large convinced that they held the answer to ensuring that all children will reach high academic levels. Their answer, at its core, is twofold. First, to have every state adopt standards backed-up by standardized tests (a process well underway). Second, to set up a system of "rewards and consequences" for teachers, students, and schools based on those tests.

Conference leaders were well aware that there is growing discontent among many teachers, students, and parents about their agenda — in particular the use of high-stakes tests as the guiding principal of education reform. (The term high-stakes tests refers to the use of a single test or battery of tests as the main and sometimes only determinant of whether a student is retained or is denied a high school diploma.) One of the clear purposes of the conference was to send a message that the discontent will not deter the governors and business leaders.

In a keynote speech riddled with terminology more appropriate for a wartime general rallying his troops, Louis Gerstner Jr., summit co-chair and IBM chairman and CEO, told participants that "it's going to be tough. Institutional change always is. But we have to bear the pain of the transition. ... We've got to have the guts and the political will to press forward."

President Clinton delivered a similar message. Adopting a framework of "tough love," he said that accountability policies that flunk children or deny them a diploma are for the child's own good. (Clinton was too smart to use the term "flunk" but instead used the wildly popular euphemism "no social promotion.")

It might be tempting to dismiss Gerstner's and Clinton's statements as political posturing with few consequences in the real world. But the summit leaders have shown they have the clout to pass legislation and influence the media in a way that guarantees, at least for now, that their vision of standards and accountability is the norm. Further, at a time of highly partisan bickering at the congressional level, the governors and corporate leaders have forged a bipartisan agreement that, while sometimes fuzzy in its details, is clear in its overall thrust. Meanwhile, progressive educators opposed to the reliance on standardized tests have not yet been able to adequately articulate an alternative system of accountability that can capture widespread public support.

"Right now, this [the governors' and business leaders'] view of standards and testing is the centerpiece of what passes for education reform," acknowledges Monty Neill, executive director of the national group FairTest. "People have to address this view very centrally."

The Summit

The meeting at the IBM headquarters was billed as the third National Education Summit. The first was in 1989, when President George Bush convened 49 of the nation's governors and established Goals 2000. (None of the goals — which ranged from wiping out adult illiteracy to making U.S. students the world's top achievers in math and science — are yet within reach.) In 1996, at the second summit, corporate leaders were brought on board and a more focused agenda was set, based on standards and accountability.

While calls for standards and accountability pre-date the 1996 summit, the governors and business leaders took the standards movement and reshaped it in their image. With calls for national standards stymied by opposition from both the right and the left, and with district and school-based efforts deemed too prone to influence from teachers and educators who conserva-

tives had decided were part of the problem, the governors and corporate leaders forged ahead on the state level. They set up state standards, often heavily influenced by conservative ideologues and think tanks. Perhaps most important, they decided that high-stakes standardized tests were the best way to determine if schools were reaching the standards.

Since 1996, the governors and corporate leaders have had an impressive track record — not so much in guaranteeing true reform and academic achievement, but in setting up their system of standards and high-stakes tests. At the time of the 1996 summit, only 14 states had established state standards in the four core academic subjects. By the next school year, 49 states will have such standards. (Iowa, which consistently scores at the top of various national academic measurements, is the only hold-out, prompting the comment from author and anti-testing advocate Alfie Kohn, "Thank God for Iowa.") Furthermore, the number of states that will be requiring students to pass high-stakes tests in order to be promoted or to graduate has jumped in the last three years from 17 to 27, and summit leaders are pushing to increase that number.

The governors and corporate leaders are quick to cite such statistics as proof of reform. On one level, that's not surprising. Both groups exist in a world where bottom-line numbers are all that mat-

Wasserman/L.A. Times Syndicate

ter: you either win an election or lose; your profits are either up or down. It seemed to escape conference leaders that the complexity of school reform cannot be so easily captured in hard-and-fast numbers.

There was a disorienting disconnect between the conference setting and the reality of most U.S. classrooms. As in 1996, the summit was held at IBM headquarters, a feudal-like conglomeration of office buildings and well-manicured grounds just north of New York City. It is a self-contained world, complete with restricted entrance (not even taxicabs were allowed onto the grounds), helicopter landing pad, swans and goldfish lazily swimming in a moat-like stream, guest hotel, and gourmet dining facilities.

For those un-attuned to IBM corporate culture, the media packet stated: "Dress for the Summit is business attire."

Little at the conference was left to chance. The draft of the final action statement was distributed weeks in advance and changed little over the course of two days. Media observers were given few opportunities to ask questions and were shuttled at night to a hotel 30 minutes away. The media were able to attend the main sessions, which consisted mostly of speeches and pre-planned questions and answers, but were barred from attending the discussion groups. Except for a few rare moments, when a Hugh Price or a Bob Chase talked to reporters in the halls, the media heard by and large what the governors and corporate leaders wanted them to hear.

As a result, the U.S. public heard mostly what the conference leaders wanted them to hear.

Summit Decisions

The "1999 Action Statement" issued at the summit's end lays out three key challenges: Improving Educator Quality; Helping All Students Achieve High Standards; and Strengthening Accountability. Each section ends with recommendations on how the three groups represented at the conference — the governors, the business leaders, and the education leaders — will meet the challenge.

The action statement makes for dry reading. But sandwiched in between the rhetoric and often-times vague phrases is an indication of how the

> *"Right now, the governors' and business leaders' view of standards and testing is the centerpiece of what passes for education reform."*
>
> — *Monty Neill, executive director of FairTest*

governors and business leaders hope to implement the next stage of their standards reform.

■ Improving Educator Quality. The action statement calls for "competitive salary structures to attract and retain the best-qualified teachers and school leaders." But the statement, unfortunately, also links resources for professional development and teacher training to "standards." (The problem is that even though the action statement does not explicitly equate standards with standardized tests, just about everything else at the conference led to that conclusion.)

The document also encourages several emerging trends such as alternative certification programs and standardized "content" tests that teachers must pass before they are certified.

In one of the most specific recommendations in the entire action plan, this section calls for merit pay plans, under which teacher salaries will be tied to student achievement.

Clearly, one of the battles ahead will be over how much teacher quality will be judged by "standards," a broad concept that can justify a variety of approaches and initiatives, and how much merely by student results on standardized tests.

■ Helping All Students Achieve High Standards. The only unequivocally positive thing that can be said about this section is that it mentions that all students must have access to high-quality instruction.

The section stresses the need for "curriculum and assessments aligned with standards." ("Alignment" was one of the summit's main buzzwords. Alas, there was no call for state budget priorities to be "aligned" with educational needs.) On the surface, aligning curriculum, assessments, and standards seems logical. The problem, however, is that because high-stakes tests are driving standards-based reform at this point, there is a growing danger that curriculum will be geared toward standardized tests, regardless of what the standards say. This raises the clear specter of classrooms across the country focusing on "teaching to the test," and, in the process, narrowing the curriculum and emphasizing memorization over critical thinking.

Nowhere does this section mention funding

The state toughened school standards again.

All student must pass test to enter bathroom

scribble scribble

John Klostner

equity or adequate resources. Instead, in an approach echoed throughout the conference, schools are told that in place of more money they will be given "substantial flexibility, freedom, and control over personnel and resources."

Most disappointing, the document lets the governors off the hook on redressing the "savage inequalities" in school funding. In fact, in looking at the various tasks assigned to conference participants in this section, there is disturbing imbalance.

■ Strengthening Accountability. The heart of the summit's approach to accountability is a system of "incentives for success and consequences for failure." Despite the nod toward the carrot of "incentives," much of the document focused on the stick of "consequences."

Throughout the conference, the consequences for low-performing students were clear: being held back or denied a diploma. Even at the conference's end, however, consequences for schools and teachers were still somewhat vague.

But one powerful political figure, presidential hopeful George W. Bush, has made clear his view of "rewards and consequences." (George W. did not attend the conference but brother Jeb, governor of Florida, did). In a statement a few days after the summit's end, George W. said that, if elected President, he would require states to annually test all students from third through eighth grade in reading and math as a condition for federal aid. States that showed progress on test scores would receive financial bonuses. States that did not show progress would lose 5% of their federal grants. Earlier, Bush had linked student testing to vouchers, saying that schools that do not make progress on state tests would have their Title I money transferred into vouchers for parents.

How long the governors and corporate leaders will be able to maintain their system of consequences remains to be seen, however, especially since their dominant strategy appears to be high-stakes tests and "no social promotion."

That idea is appealing in the abstract and parents seem to support it — for now. But what will happen when hundreds of thousands of kids are flunked or denied a high school diploma? As C. Thomas Holmes, a University of Georgia education professor who is a leading researcher on the topic, notes: "Parents are all for retention, until it's their kid." ❏

— *Barbara Miner is managing editor of Rethinking Schools.*

The above is condensed from an article that appeared in Rethinking Schools, Vol. 14, #2, Winter 1999/2000.

The full text is available at www.rethinkingschools.org, go to "Past Isues."

Responding to Test-Driven Reform

In response to the standards and testing movement, several approaches are emerging. Some argue that progressives should concentrate on using the rhetoric of "high standards for all" to reopen the discussion on "opportunity to learn standards" — that is, providing sufficient resources and "opportunities to learn" before instituting across-the-board expectations for results. Others emphasize the importance of legal action and filing suit against high-stakes tests on civil rights grounds. In Chicago, for example, a civil rights complaint has been filed against the Chicago district's "no social promotion" policy on the grounds that the policy disproportionately affects African-American and Latino students.

Many progressive educators emphasize a stance of active resistance and, where appropriate, of boycotting the tests and adopting a "just say no" approach. A number of parents, teachers, and students, particularly in Massachusetts, Illinois, and California, have been organizing along these lines.

As Monty Neill of FairTest argues, "Should you go along with the dominant definition of reform, or do you fight it if you think it is an educational disaster? And I think it is an educational disaster."

In addition to active resistance, Neill highlights two other important tasks: to demand better and more authentic methods of public accountability, and to develop high quality classroom-based assessments that can help teachers better teach.

Theresa Perry, vice president for community relations at Wheelock College in Boston, argues that many African-American educators and parents are leery of a "just say no" approach and worry that the African-American community can't wait forever for better assessments to come along. She underscores the need to help African-American students pass the tests, and to use the tests to redress the chronic problem of low expectations and sub-standard curriculum for many African-American students.

> "Should you go along with the dominant definition of reform, or do you fight it if you think it is an educational disaster? And I think it is an educational disaster."
>
> — Monty Neill of FairTest

"Fundamentally, the only way you can gain access to opportunity is by passing through these gatekeeping tests," she said. "Unless the tests are going to go away tomorrow, the real issue is, how do you…help poor kids to pass the test?"

"The tests are flawed, but what is the alternative?" she continues. "And are the White progressives willing to take a stand in their local community to equalize outcomes?"

Michael Apple, an education policy professor at the University of Wisconsin-Madison, stresses the importance of a dual stance. While it's important to recognize that the tests are not going to go away anytime soon, he said, one must still point out "how these things have worked historically. That is, they exacerbate social problems, they blame the same students, teachers, and parents who have been blamed before, and they serve as an excuse not to equalize material resources."

Apple cautioned that progressives who are opposed to high-stakes tests must be careful not to allow themselves to be painted as anti-reform and as defenders of the status quo. "The idea is to think strategically," he said, "and not to form a rejectionist front that allows your enemies to position you in a way that makes you even less powerful."

Asa Hilliard, professor of urban education at Georgia State University, argues that, "For the segment of the community that doesn't have power, the worst thing they can do is to drop out of the game and not take the test," he said. But, he adds, after helping kids pass the test, "you have to then turn right around and challenge the tests."

Asked for what's the best way forward, Hilliard summed up the problem this way: "I don't think there's a magic solution. The problem is, the people who are advocating the high-stakes tests believe that they have the solution. And they are going to make consequences based on that."

— Barbara Miner

The Jobs of Tomorrow

In his keynote speech to the National Education Summit, IBM chairman and CEO, Louis Gerstner Jr., repeatedly stressed that the jobs of tomorrow will be in high-skill, high-wage occupations. "Jobs that today require low-to-moderate skills — and pay low-to-moderate wages — are in decline, while demand soars for highly skilled applicants who command higher pay," Gerstner said.

Figures from the Bureau of Labor Statistics' "Employment Projections 1996-2006" show a different story. In fact, jobs merely requiring short or moderate on-the-job training, such as clerical and service jobs, will account for more than half of all jobs in 2006.

"Employers will hire more than three times as many cashiers as engineers," columnist Richard Rothstein noted in an article in the Oct. 27 *New York Time*s. "They will need more than twice as many food-counter workers, waiters, and waitresses than all the systems analysts, computer engineers, mathematicians, and database administrators combined. We will be hiring more nurses, but even more janitors and maids."

One of the sources of confusion is that while professions such as computer engineering will increase percentage-wise, the number is relatively small to begin with. So, as Rothstein notes, one can proclaim that computer engineering and science employment "will increase by a whopping 100% while food service grows by only 11%. But computer science is a relatively small field, so new positions generate rapid growth rates. There are more waitresses today, so smaller percentage growth yields more new jobs."

It's also important to realize that high-skilled jobs are subject to a fluctuating supply and demand that has as much to do with corporate profits than education — as Gerstner well realizes.

Gerstner came to IBM in 1993 (his previous corporate post was head of RJR Nabisco, where he helped oversee the Joe Camel campaign which made Camels the most prominent cigarette among children.) In line with the corporate downsizing then sweeping the nation, he fired 90,000 highly trained employees, about one-third of IBM's workforce. "That was in addition to the other 183,000 quality employees that IBM fired before Gerstner arrived," notes Clinton Boutwell in his book *Shell Game: Corporate America's Agenda for Schools* (Phi Delta Kappa, 1997).

— *Barbara Miner*

The Educational Costs Of Standardization

More testing might sound nice as a policy soundbite. But as Texas shows, the move toward high-stakes tests shortchanges learning in the classroom.

BY
LINDA MCNEIL

Editor's Note: The following article examines how high-stakes testing has affected teaching and learning in classrooms in Houston, the fifth largest public school system in the United States.

Texas is the second largest state, and its educational policies help set the national agenda. Furthermore, Texas has been cited, particularly by backers of presidential hopeful and Texas Governor George W. Bush, as a positive example of how high-stakes testing can act as a catalyst of education reform. Under the Texas Assessment of Academic Skills (TAAS), students cannot graduate if they fail the TAAS exams. Further, a principal's pay is tied to the school's performance on TAAS.

The following article provides an overview of how an emphasis on high-stakes testing affects teaching and learning in the classroom — particularly in schools with large percentages of African-American and Latino students who have traditionally scored lower on standardized tests than White students in more affluent areas.

The article is condensed from the final chapter of the book Contradictions of School Reform: The Educational Costs of Standardized Testing. *The book is based on research by Linda McNeil at a set of magnet schools. She visited the schools prior to the implementation of centralized accountability measures and then again after the reforms were imposed, documenting the effects on classroom practice.* ❑

The town's head librarian loved to encourage the children of his small, isolated farming community to read. He frequently went to the local school to read to the children. Most recently, he had been reading to a class of "at-risk" eighth-graders — students who had been held back two or more years in school. They loved his reading and his choices of books. He reports feeling very frustrated: the department chair has told him not to come any more to read to the students — they are too busy preparing for their TAAS test.
— unsolicited correspondence

Three in a row? No, No, No!
[Three answers "b" in a row? No, No, No!]
— one of several cheers taught to students at their daily pep rallies on test-taking strategies for the TAAS test.

In many urban schools, particularly those whose students are predominantly poor and minority, the TAAS system of testing reduces both the quality of what is taught and the quantity of what is taught. Because the principal's pay (and job contract) and the school's reputation depend on the school's scores, in those schools where students have traditionally not tested well on standardized tests, the regular curriculum in these subjects is frequently set aside in order that students can prepare for the test.

Reading skills, writing, and math are currently being tested by

TAAS. Common sense would suggest that if a teacher followed a traditional curriculum, even using the state's textbook, the teaching of regular lessons would be preparation for success on the test. If students were able to do math problems, explain math concepts, and apply math skills in the regular sequence of lessons, then it should follow that they would do well on the test.

The tests, however, are not necessarily consistent with traditional teaching and learning. First, they are multiple-choice; they call for selecting among given answers. Second, they call for accurately darkening a circle beside the selected answer, without making stray marks on the paper.

In minority schools, in the urban school district where the magnet schools are located, and in many schools across the state, substantial class time is spent practicing bubbling in answers and learning to recognize "distractor" (obviously incorrect) answers. Students are drilled on such strategies as the one in the pep rally cheer quoted above: if you see you have answered "b" three times in a row, you know ("no, no, no") that at least one of those answers is likely to be wrong, because the maker of a test would not be likely to construct three questions in a row with the same answer-indicator. (The basis for such advice comes from the publishers of test-prep materials, many of whom send consultants into schools — for a substantial price — to help plan pep rallies, to "train" teachers to use the TAAS-prep kits, and to ease the substitution of their TAAS-prep materials for the curriculum in classrooms where teachers stubbornly resist.)

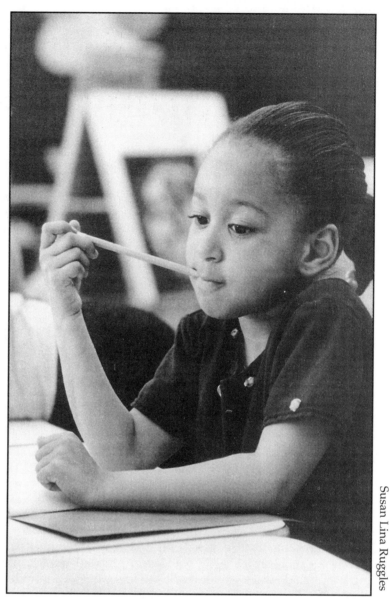

Susan Lina Ruggles

Less Latitude

Teachers, even those who know their subjects and their students well, have much less latitude when their principals purchase test-prep materials to be used in lieu of the regular curriculum.

One teacher, a graduate of an Ivy League college, with a master's degree at another select college, had spent considerable time and money assembling a rich collection of historical and literary works of importance in Latino culture. She had sought titles especially related to the Ameri-

can Southwest for her classes at a Latino high school. Her building of a classroom resource collection was extremely important given the school's lack of a library and its lean instructional budget. Her students responded to her initiative with a real enthusiasm to study and learn. She was dismayed to see, upon returning one day from lunch, that the books for her week's lessons had been set aside. In the center of her desk was a stack of test-prep booklets with a teacher's guide and a note saying "use these instead of your regular curriculum until after the TAAS." The TAAS test date was three months away. (The prep materials bore the logo "Guerrilla TAAS," as in making war on the TAAS test; the booklet covers were military-camouflage colors; the Guerrilla TAAS consultants came to the school in camouflage gear to do a TAAS pep rally for the students and faculty.) This teacher reported that her principal, a person dedi-

Jean-Claude Lejeune

cated to these students and to helping them pass the TAAS in order to graduate, had spent almost $20,000, virtually the entire instructional budget for the year, on these materials. The cost was merely one problem. Inside the booklets for "reading" were single-page activities, with brief reading selections followed by TAAS-type answer choices. These students, who had been analyzing the poetry of Gary Soto and exploring the generational themes in *Bless Me Última*, had to set aside this intellectual work to spend more than half of every class period working through the TAAS-prep booklet.

Teachers in urban schools say that to raise questions about the TAAS and about artificial test prep is characterized as being against minority students' chances to get high test scores. Or it is portrayed as "not being a team player." The test scores generated by centralized, standardized tests like the TAAS, and by the test-prep materials which prepare them for those tests, are not reliable indicators of learning. It is here where the effects on low-performing students, particularly minority students, begin to skew the possibilities for their access to a richer education.

At this school and other minority high schools where TAAS prep is replacing the curriculum, teachers report that even though many more students are passing TAAS "reading," few of their students are actually readers. Few of them can use reading for assignments in literature, science, or history classes; few of them choose to read; few of them can make meaning of literature or connect writing and discussing to reading. In schools where TAAS reading scores are going up, there is little or no will to address this gap. In fact, the rise in scores is used to justify even more TAAS prep, even more pep rallies, even more substituting of test-based programs for the regular curriculum.

TAAS and Reading

Advocates of TAAS might argue that passing the reading skills section of TAAS is better than not being able to read at all. However, there is first of all no evidence that these students "cannot read at all." Second, teachers are reporting that the kind of test prep frequently done to raise test scores may actually hamper students' ability to learn to read for meaning outside the test setting. In fact, students report that in the drills on the TAAS reading section, they frequently mark answers without reading the sample of text. They merely match key words in an answer choice with key words in the text. The definition of "reading" as captured on the test ignores a broad and sophisticated research base on the teaching of reading and on children's development as language learners. When teachers are able to draw on this professional knowledge base, it does not lead them to testing formats like TAAS for help with their children's reading.

Elementary teachers have expressed the concern that extensive prep for the reading section of TAAS actually undermines children's ability to read sustained passages. The prep materials in reading, again purchased by principals eager to protect their performance contract or perhaps to help children pass the test, feature brief passages. After reading a passage, students are to answer practice questions ("Which of the following is the main idea?" "Which of the following would not make a good title for this paragraph?" "Which of the following was described as ' ... '?"). The selected passage is not something they will see again; it is not even linked to the subsequent practice passage.

Students who practice these reading exercises day after day for months (many principals have teachers begin TAAS prep in September and do not let them revert to the "regular" curriculum until after the TAAS test in March) show a decreased ability to read longer works. A sixth-grade teacher who had selected a fourth-grade Newbery Award book for her class, thinking all the students could read and understand it, found that after reading for a few minutes the students stopped. They were accustomed to reading very brief, disjointed passages; they had difficulty carrying over information from the first chapter to a later one. Discussions with other upper elementary and middle school teachers confirm that students accustomed to TAAS prep, rather than literature, may be internalizing the format of reading skills tests but not the habits needed to read for meaning.

TAAS and Writing

The teaching of "writing," also a subject tested by TAAS, has been reduced in many schools to daily practice of the essay form being tested that year. A teacher who is African-American and always alert to good educational opportunities for her sons was very pleased that her second son

One teacher was given a stack of test-prep materials with the note: "Use these until after the TAAS." The test was three months away.

would be able to have the same excellent fourth-grade teacher under whom her oldest son had thrived. She was not prepared for the TAAS-based transformation of the fourth grade in the intervening years. She said that although the principal and teacher remained the same, the entire fourth-grade curriculum had been replaced by TAAS prep. Writing had become daily practice in "the persuasive essay," consisting of five five-sentence paragraphs, a form which clearly qualifies as "school knowledge" in the most limited sense. What students had to say in these essays was of virtually no importance; conforming to the form was the requirement, and the students practiced every day. This mother knew that in Anglo schools, while there was some abuse of teaching through TAAS prep, most of the children were nevertheless learning to tailor their writing to their subjects, write in different voices and formats to different audiences, write to stretch their vocabularies.

A principal of a middle- to upper-middle-class elementary school explained to an audience at a school reform conference that her teachers had heard that teachers at other schools were having their students practice the five-paragraph essay every day. They were concerned to hear that it had become the only form of writing done that year in their school. This principal, under much less pressure to contrive passing rates for her students on the TAAS, worked with her teachers to include the TAAS as one of many "audiences" when they teach students to develop voice and a sense of audience in their writing. Similarly, several high school teachers have told of discussions they had with their students about the TAAS writing exam. After learning more about TAAS, the students decided to think of the audience for their TAAS writing test as "bureaucrats sitting in little offices, waiting to count sentences and paragraphs." These teachers, usually in high-performing schools and therefore not required to do TAAS prep, are in a similar way trying to make the test the subject of critical inquiry. This is not typical in low-performing schools where teachers and principals are using pep rallies and incentive prizes to get students to "buy in" to these forms of evaluation.

The younger children growing up with TAAS prep may not always know (unless they compare with friends in private schools or have an older sibling whose learning was more substantive) how TAAS-prep reading and writing differ from good instruction. Older children, however, are not without skepticism that this system of testing is altering what they and their teachers jointly regard as important learning. Elaine, an eighth-grader, knows firsthand the artificiality of "TAAS writing." In a previous grade, she won the city-wide short-story writing award conferred by the local chapter of the National Council of Teachers of English. The next spring she received notice that she failed to pass the eighth-grade writing section of the TAAS because she "failed to provide sufficient supporting detail." Elaine and her teacher both know that she is known in her school as a writer. What distinguishes her writing is its rich detail. They could speculate that perhaps the scanning of her TAAS writing missed, by its haste or its rigid format, the elaborative and "supporting" detail that characterizes her writing. The TAAS, and not the quality of her writing nor the English teachers' judgment, lost credibility for her and for her parents as an indicator of her writing skills.

Teachers who question the test-prep for TAAS are criticized as "not being a team player."

Intellectual Subtraction

An eighth-grade class in a predominantly poor, Latino middle school demonstrated pointedly the intellectual subtraction resulting from the TAAS system of testing when the emphasis is on raising minority scores. In mid-September, a group of community visitors stepped into Mr. Sanchez's class just as he was covering the blackboard with rules for semicolon usage. Using semicolons in writing seemed a useful and worthy lesson for eighth-graders working on their writing, so at first the visitors watched without comment. While the students were copying the semicolon rules, the teacher explained: "We are having to do grammar until after the TAAS. I'm so excited — this year we have a whole nine weeks after the TAAS to do eighth-grade English. I always do Shakespeare with my students. And I have many stories that they love to read. Last year we didn't have much time, but this year I will have a whole nine weeks." The visitors were just then realizing the import of his words: he was to do TAAS prep from September until March, and then "teach eighth-grade English" only in the remaining nine weeks. And the teacher was made to feel grateful for all nine of those weeks. He

explained that it was the will of the principal that they get the scores up and that everyone in the school was feeling the pressure. He knew that by focusing on the TAAS alone, his students would be getting far less than the eighth-grade curriculum studied by students in schools where the student demographics (middle class, predominantly White) would carry the scores, and they would be learning even less than his own students in the years before TAAS.

TAAS and Math

Under the TAAS-prep system, the teaching of mathematics, the third subject currently tested, is also highly truncated. TAAS tests math by having students choose among four or five possible answers. They are not asked to explain their answers, so if students have alternative ways of working a problem, their reasoning is not made visible on the test. Nor are their reasons for selecting "correct" answers. Being able to conceptualize in mathematics, being able to envision a solution and select among possible approaches, being able to articulate the reasoning behind the answer — none of these is tested by TAAS. TAAS tests computational accuracy and familiarity with basic operations. The reductive mathematics on the test is not adequate preparation for courses in more advanced mathematics. The TAAS-prep booklets, which emphasize test-taking strategies over mathematical reasoning, again create a gap between the content learned by poor and minority students in schools investing in TAAS-prep kits and the students in well-provisioned schools. In these latter schools, principals assume students will pass because of their family background and their having attended "good" schools in lower grades. They therefore support the teaching of the regular academic curriculum without substantial risk that to do so might "lower" the TAAS scores.

Circumventing TAAS

If a teacher wanted to avoid TAAS prep and focus on the students and the curriculum, then it would seem that the answer would be to teach a subject not yet tested by TAAS. At the Pathfinder school, Ms. Bartlett had claimed a space for teaching complex biology topics by shifting some of her teaching out from under the controls of the proficiency system (the predecessor of TAAS). She created elective courses and independent study

seminars around such units of study as ecology and habitats (enabling her to integrate concepts and topics that were fragmented and sequenced separately under the proficiencies). She taught a biochemistry elective (using her knowledge gained from the medical school mentorship and crossing traditional subject boundaries) and, in some semesters, marine biology. Under the TAAS system of testing, teachers report that there are fewer and fewer venues in which they can do authentic teaching, even though officially only three subjects — math, reading, and writing — are tested. In poor and minority schools, especially, teaching untested subjects such as art, science, or social studies is not exempt from the pressures of TAAS prep. An art teacher with a reputation for engaging her Latino students in serious studio work, and for exciting students about being in school, was required to suspend the teaching of art in order to drill her students daily in TAAS grammar. By the time the grammar drills were completed, there was no time to set up for art projects. Her students were doubly losing: their treatment of grammar was artificial, aimed at correctness within the multiple-choice format of the test, rather than at fluency in their own writing; and they were denied an opportunity to develop their sense of color and design in art.

Distorting Teaching

A history teacher in an under-resourced Latino high school worked with his colleagues to create a history curriculum that would maintain authentic content and yet incorporate some of the skills their students would need to do well on the TAAS. They included the writing of essays on historical topics and attention to reading skills. They had at first been given permission to create this on their own but later were told that they needed to set aside the teaching of history entirely in order to "cooperate with the rest of the faculty" in getting students to pass the TAAS. This history teacher's assignment was to drill his students every day on

math, a subject outside his field of expertise.

Science teachers who have spent a year in the Rice University Center for Education Model Science Lab (located in an urban middle school) updating their science knowledge and upgrading their capacity for laboratory-based teaching enter the program with the consent of their principals to implement what they have learned when they return to their schools. Many of these teachers have discovered on returning to their home schools that they are required, for as much as two to four months of the school year, to suspend the teaching of science in order to drill students on TAAS math. Again, their students in these urban schools are doubly penalized, first for losing out on the science that their peers in suburban schools are learning. Second, they are penalized by having to spend extra periods on low-level, disjointed math drills — math divorced from both the applications and conceptual understandings they will need if they are to hold their own later in upper-level math classes with middle-class students. It is unlikely that the middle-class students have been doing "math" from commercial test-prep booklets, rather than from math books, manipulatives, calculators, computers, and peer study groups. The TAAS, then, lowers the quality and quantity of even subjects not being tested in those schools where students have traditionally not tested well, the students who are poor and the minority. ❐

— *Linda McNeil is co-director of the Center for Education at Rice University and a professor of education. She is author of Contradictions of Control: School Structure and School Knowledge.*

©2000 by Routledge. Reprinted with permission.
The above appeared in Rethinking Schools,
Vol. 14, #4, Summer 2000.

Racial Bias Built into Texas Test

The Texas system of high-stakes tests, known as the Texas Assessment of Academic Skills (TAAS) presents an example of how racial bias can be built into standardized tests.

In an unsuccessful suit arguing that the TAAS tests were unconstitutional because they discriminated against students of color, the judge concluded that he "cannot quarrel" with the finding that bias is embedded in the test.

Professor Martin Shapiro of Emory University had explained that the TAAS test uses "point-biserial correlations" in deciding which items to use and which items to discard when constructing the test.

Under this process, preference is given to items on a preliminary field test that were answered correctly by high-scoring test-takers. Such questions are said to have a high biserial correlation. Items answered correctly by low-scoring students, which have a low biserial correlation, tend to be discarded. This is part of a process of trying to ensure "technical reliability" — that the test results for an individual or group at two different testings be as close as possible.

Under the process of "point-biserial correlation," items that produce the greatest gap between high and low scorers are most often used. Because students of color tend to perform less well on the test as a whole, the effort to increase reliability increases bias against students of color — the questions they tend to answer correctly are the questions that tend to get thrown out.

Testing to Sort Students

Biserial correlation measures were developed to be used in tests which are designed to sort and rank students. However, tests such as the TAAS now rely on biserial correlations, even though the TAAS is supposedly not intended to sort students but to determine whether they have met specified levels of achievement. Yet biserial correlation helps ensure that at least some students who know the material and ought to pass the tests do not. These students are overwhelmingly low-income, of color, use English as a second language, or have special needs.

Alternatives exist. One would be to reject the underlying assumption of "uni–dimensionality," on which point-biserial correlations rest. In this approach, test-makers assume that test-taker performance can be described by a single underlying ability.

This approach has two major problems. First, it assumes that performance on the many sub-topics in a subject, such as algebra and geometry in math, is due to one, not multiple and possibly different abilities. Second, uni–dimensionality in test items assumes that test takers employ only one cognitive process to solve a problem, rather than multiple modes of thinking which can interact in varied ways.

Human development and use of cognitive processes can vary based on social and cultural background. If a test assumes uni–dimensionality of cognitive processes — and the "acceptable" processes include only some culturally based approaches — then the test becomes culturally biased. Bias review techniques which use point-biserial correlations, as most do, will not detect this flaw. ❏

> ## QUOTABLE QUOTE
>
> **"Clearly, MCAS [Massachusetts Comprehensive Assessment System] exams should be abolished. We support higher standards, but we don't support impediments. When you put a high stakes test that is not applicable to all students, clearly it is a discriminatory act."**
>
> *— Leonard Alkins, Boston president of the National Association for the Advancement of Colored People. Alkins made the comment after 80% of Black and 85% of Latino 10th graders failed the MCAS math test in May 2000, compared to 45% of Whites.*

— *The above is adapted from an article in the Winter 1999-2000 issue of the FairTest Examiner.*

Testing Corporations

Writing and administering standardized tests is a big money-maker for a handful of companies.

Standardized testing is a big business, worth hundreds of millions of dollars to the handful of corporations that dominate the testing market.

States and districts often turn to testing companies to write, score, and interpret the standardized tests given students. One reason is that it is cheaper and easier to buy an "off-the-shelf" test than to develop a test at the district or state level.

While the educational merits of standardized tests are highly controversial, no one disputes that the testing companies are coming out clear winners. "What once was a quiet, though productive, niche has exploded into a booming and lucrative industry," notes Stephen Hegarty in an article June 19, 2000 in the *St. Petersburg Times*.

The testing companies do not release specific financial data. But the testing market was estimated at $218.7 million in 1999 by the Association of American Publishers, according to an analysis by the Grassroots Innovative Policy Program (GRIPP), a nationwide network of progressive policy groups. Revenues are growing at about 9% a year, significantly higher than for the educational publishing industry as a whole.

Top Players

The four top players in the testing business are:

■ National Computer Systems of Minneapolis. The smallest of the major testing companies, NCS first just scored tests but now writes them as well. The company reported $629 million in revenue this year, double its figure from 1996. It recently landed the testing contract for Florida, worth $122 million over five years, according to Hegarty.

■ CTB/McGraw-Hill of Monterey, CA. Like the other three testing giants, CTB is an arm of a major textbook publisher, in this case McGraw-Hill. The company publishes the TerraNova test, variations of which are used throughout the country, from California, to Wisconsin, to New York.

■ Harcourt Brace of San Antonio. Harcourt is the parent company of the Psychological Corporation, which makes the Stanford Achievement Test — often called the Stanford-9. This test has existed in different forms for nearly 80 years. Harcourt recently won a five-year contract in California worth $12 million a year, according to GRIPP. Harcourt has testing contracts with about two dozen states, according to an April 9, 2000 article in the Education Life supplement to *The New York Times*.

■ Riverside Publishing, owned by Houghton Mifflin and based in Itasca, IL. Smaller than Harcourt or CTB, Riverside makes the popular Iowa Test of Basic Skills, extensively used to test elementary-age children.

There are also companies that publish test-prep books, consisting of sample practice tests, test-taking strategies, and study aids.

The Princeton Review, for example, recently announced development of test-prep guides for the Texas Assessment of Academic Skills. The series includes six books costing $17 each.

The Princeton Review, known for its test-prep books for the SAT and ACT tests, publishes a similar series for New York and has titles forthcoming for the Virginia standards and the Massachusetts standards. Princeton Review is a division of Random House publishers. ❐

— Barbara Miner

> ## QUOTABLE QUOTE
>
> "'Accountability' usually turns out to be a code for tighter control over what happens in classrooms by people who are not in classrooms — and has approximately the same effect on learning that a noose has on breathing."
>
> *— Author and anti-testing activist Alfie Kohn*

Why Business Likes More Testing

Standardized tests serve important functions, which is one reason they are not likely to disappear any time soon.

BY ARTHUR MACEWAN

More testing and the standardization of standards — if not higher standards — serves a couple of important functions.

Aside from whatever role the schools actually play in educating people, businesses have long looked to the schools to serve a sorting function, separating those students who persevere and achieve from those who do not. Firms look to the schools not so much for skill creation, as for preparing students to learn the specific skills they need on the job. The firms will usually do the training, but it helps them to know who is ready to be trained.

If the schools' sorting process is effective, then, when a firm hires a person with a high school diploma or an associate's degree, the firm knows what that means. If the schools do their job well, they eliminate a costly step in the hiring process.

Yet businesses are bothered when they do not know what a particular degree or diploma means, when it may not mean that the sorting process has been at all effective. Moreover, operating in a national job market, firms would like to have the same degree mean the same thing regardless of location. Standardization of standards is unlikely to affect what goes on in the schools and is therefore unlikely to do any good for the students. Yet, even if the "product" of the schools is in no way improved, standardization of the "product" is useful for the buyers.

Also, standardized testing is increasingly important as our society becomes increasingly unequal. Inequality can survive only if people believe it has some legitimacy. The schools teach many things, but the more they use standardized testing, the more they teach the lesson that performance on tests is a legitimate way to establish social hierarchy.

> *The more that schools use standardized testing, the more they teach that performance on tests is a legitimate way to establish social hierarchy.*

We like to believe that we live in a meritocracy, that those people who are at the top got there because of their abilities. From this belief it is a short step — though one without any logic at all — to the conclusion that the people on top deserve to be on top.

The grading and testing systems of schools are important steps in the creation and re-creation of this essential set of ideas. In performing this function, test and standards help preserve the status quo, but they do nothing to improve the education or lives of most people.

Business Needs

What business wants from the schools is a populace that accepts the status quo and a work force ready to meet its needs.

There is much talk about "new technology" creating the need for a work force of problem solvers, people who can work in groups, and people with more extensively developed cognitive skills. At the same time, business wants what it has always wanted — people who will follow the rules.

In a 1994 article extolling the virtues of Motorola as an employer with a "commitment to employees learning," *Business Week* summed up the issues in an interesting manner. In Motorola's initiative for training and the development of skills among its workers, "The goal is a work force that is disciplined yet free thinking.

The initiative will aim to inculcate them with company procedures so they're a well-oiled machine but also to develop the knowledge and independent mindedness that Motorola will need to conquer rapidly changing technologies and markets."

The same contradictory message permeates the recent and important book by Richard Murnane and Frank Levy, *Teaching the New Basic Skills: Principles for Educating Children to Thrive in a Changing Economy*. Murnane and Levy argue that changing technology has created a situation where people entering the labor force need a new set of basic skills if they are to be able to earn a "middle-class wage."

New Basic Skills

In addition to "high school level" reading and math ability, these new basic skills include: capacities for problem identification and problem solving, oral communication, and teamwork. But there is one more set of "skills" that Murnane and Levy clearly have in mind, though they don't include it explicitly on their list (perhaps because they take it for granted), namely the skills needed to fit in, to be a "team player," to follow company rules, to be ready for overtime when needed, to identify with the company, and give paramount attention to the goal of "productivity."

U.S. firms, however, not only need quiescent and cooperative workers who possess the "new

> *"Bad" schools are not dysfunctional. They are performing an important social function of channeling people into the lowest levels of employment.*

basic skills," workers who might receive a "middle-class wage." They also need workers who will fill the bottom tiers of the occupational hierarchy. In spite of the fact that many low wage manufacturing jobs are now located in poor countries, there are numerous jobs that do not require the new basic skills but which cannot be moved abroad. Food service workers and janitors, two of the job categories that are expected to provide the largest number of new jobs during the current decade, are good examples.

Not all of these jobs can be filled by teenagers and recent immigrants. As long as these sorts of jobs exist, as long as we have a multi-tiered, segmented job market, U.S. firms will have a need for the people who go to the "bad" schools. These schools are not dysfunctional, as they so often are presented by well-meaning critics, but are performing an important function of channeling people into the lowest levels of employment. Some may get channeled right out of the system entirely, but, if we build prison cells fast enough, they should present no real problem." ❑

— Arthur MacEwan teaches economics at the University of Massachusetts — Boston and was a founding editor of Dollars & Sense magazine.

The above is excerpted from Radical Teacher Number 51. Reprinted with permission.

Is There Value in Value-Added Testing?

Milwaukee plans an unprecedented expansion in standardized testing, amid fears that its innovative performance assessments will disappear as a districtwide accountability measure.

BY BOB PETERSON

The following article provides an in-depth look at how test-driven reform is unfolding in one urban district, and how it is edging out more progressive forms of assessment.

The Milwaukee School Board appears poised to embark on an unprecedented expansion of standardized testing — despite warnings from experts on assessment; lack of input from parents, teachers, and principals; and a single public hearing held three business days after details of the expansion were released.

The proposal calls for almost tripling the number of standardized tests given to Milwaukee Public School (MPS) students. The overriding concern is that teachers will be pressured to focus on memorization and low-level skills rather than on encouraging students to think more critically, analytically, and in depth — the kind of learning not easily measured by a computerized, fill-in-the-bubble standardized test.

Milwaukee's plan is part of a national trend to increase school accountability through reliance on standardized tests. In Milwaukee, a key argument is that the district needs better longitudinal data on student performance.

But the dilemma in MPS, as in other urban districts, is not the inability to produce data but rather how best to promote academic achievement. "We don't need to have further documentation of failure," notes Beverly Cross, Professor of Urban Education at University of Wisconsin-Milwaukee and a *Rethinking Schools* editor. "What we need are programs that push teachers to be more effective and creative in their teaching."

Critics of the MPS proposal are particularly upset that the plan calls for standardized testing beginning in kindergarten — despite warnings that testing at a young age is educationally inappropriate and may actually harm young children.

The main criticism of the proposal, which is formally called a "Balanced Assessment System," is the massive increase in standardized testing and its effect on teaching and learning, especially in early grades. Critics raise three other important problems.

■ First, MPS is pushing the proposal with undue haste and a lack of democratic input. "This proposal touches the heart of the educational process," Mary Diez, graduate dean at Milwaukee's Alverno College and a national expert on assessment, wrote in a letter to the MPS School Board. "Shouldn't parents, teachers, and others in the public who are concerned with the quality of public education be able to help shape the plan?"

■ Second, the plan calls for "replacing the district performance assessments." MPS has been a national leader in district wide performance assessments in which students are evaluated on concrete activities such as written essays, science experiments, or oral presentations. Under the proposal, performance assessments would exist instead in some undefined manner at the local school and classroom levels. "The enormous danger is that performance assessments will simply go away," Cynthia Ellwood, principal of Hartford Avenue University School and former Director of Education Services in MPS, told *Rethinking Schools*. "The pressures will be so great within schools not to administer performance assessments in an era of decentralization that they will essentially disappear."

■ Third, the plan does not even mention how the standardized testing will affect students with special needs, or students who do not speak English as their first language, or students in Milwaukee's nationally acclaimed language immersion schools where young children receive virtually all their instruction in French, German, or Spanish.

The Proposal's Essentials

The MPS proposal relies on a concept of longitudinal testing known as "value-added assessments," devised by William Sanders, a professor of statistics at the University of Tennessee. This approach is nominally designed to see how much "educational value" has been added to a student during a given time. It is especially popular in Tennessee, Texas, and North Carolina.

The heart of the MPS proposal is an increased emphasis on standardized testing and a decreased emphasis on performance-based assessments. Under the plan, an MPS student would take 52 standardized tests during their kinder- garten through high school career, compared to the 19 standardized tests a student currently takes.

Presently, the first standardized test administered district wide is the Wisconsin Reading Comprehension Test, (also known as Third Grade Reading Test) as part of a statewide mandate. MPS students also currently take the state-mandated standardized tests that are given in six academic subjects in fourth, eighth, and 10th grades. These tests, known as the Wisconsin Student Assessment System (WSAS) tests or Terra Nova tests, are developed by the publishing conglomerate McGraw-Hill. Beginning in 2004, state law requires that the district administer a high school graduation test.

The new MPS plan adds yearly standardized tests in four academic areas (math, writing, language arts, and reading) for students in first, second, third, fifth, sixth, seventh and ninth grades — the grades not covered by the statewide test. In kindergarten students will be given a reading test. Thus, students will take standardized tests in every grade. This expansion is not required by the state.

The new testing proposal also calls for "replacing the district performance assessments" as a measure of the district's overall performance.

Currently, MPS has district wide performance assessments that are given to all students. They were implemented in recent years in writing in fourth, fifth, eighth, and 10th grades. Eventually, performance assessments were added in science,

The proposal relies on the concept of "value-added assessment" — to see how much "educational value" has been added to a student during a given time.

math, oral language, and the arts.

While not without problems, performance assessments tend to be more educationally beneficial because they are tied to improving classroom teaching and learning, and to demonstrating that students can perform activities that are of use in the real world. Standardized tests, in contrast, focus on ranking students.

Monty Neill, executive director of the National Center for Fair & Open Testing (FairTest) in Cambridge, MA, has been involved in evaluating Milwaukee's existing assessments. He calls the testing proposal a big step backward.

"Milwaukee has been a leader in developing more authentic forms of assessment," he told *Rethinking Schools*. "It's a pity that the district doesn't build on what you have here. Once again, we are seeing a reduction of all the outcomes of schooling to what can be measured on standardized tests, the most simplistic form of assessment."

Pros and cons

The main arguments for the new testing program fall into three areas:

■ The need to have better longitudinal data on students' academic achievement.

■ The need to recognize that kids begin school at different places and grow at different rates.

■ The need to remove performance assessments as district-mandated school accountability measures.

Need for Longitudinal Data

The MPS proposal says that the "value-added" testing system will "inform students, parents, school sites, the district, and the general public as to how much educational value has been added through the learning experience during a given period of time." It argues that even if all students do not perform the same, the schools should at least be able to show that some "value" has been added.

Kay Mantilla, Acting Director of the MPS Division of Research and Assessment, said the new tests would give "parents the knowledge of how their children are progressing outside the confines of a report card because our report cards are so diverse in Milwaukee." She also said the data would be used mainly for "diagnostic purposes," because teachers would get an "item analysis" of what students missed on the test.

At the School Board committee hearing, board member John Gardner said he also wanted the data to be able to "distinguish [and] evaluate ... the accomplishments of schools, programs, and most importantly teachers that are effective."

Critics of the new testing program have several responses. First, the value-added standardized tests are very limited in what they measure. "The idea of seeing

how kids do over time is reasonable, but you have to have good measures," Neill of FairTest argues. "The standardized tests don't tell you enough about what is really going on with a student's learning."

Second, the district already documents which schools and students are having difficulties, using standardized tests, district wide performance assessments, and measures such as dropouts, attendance, and graduation rates.

Further, there are a number of classroom assessments that can be used to show student progress or the lack thereof. Milwaukee elementary school teachers, for example, are required to individually and formally assess students' reading levels twice a year by having students read to the teacher and answer comprehension questions. Many teachers give end-of-chapter or end-of-unit tests in various subjects. Report cards are issued four or six times a year and parent conferences are held twice a year.

Given existing standardized tests, performance assessments, individual reading inventories, report cards, and parent conferences, there are adequate data for parents and teachers. In fact, those data are a much better reflection of a child's academic strengths and weaknesses than a once-a-year test. As for schoolwide accountability, the district's annual *Accountability Report* provides a

great deal of data to indicate which schools are relatively more successful than others.

Students begin school at different levels. Advocates of value-added testing argue that because kids begin schools with different levels of knowledge and skills, it's not fair to hold up one bar or standard for them to meet. Instead, advocates argue, each student should be expected to grow at different rates and be judged accordingly. Professor Sanders, credited with creating the complex statistical model to measure such "value-added" growth, explained this point in the May 2000 issue of *Teacher* magazine: "I believe we should visualize the curriculum not as stair steps, but rather as a ramp. I want all kids to go up the ramp, but I recognize that not all kids are going to be at the same place at the same time. What I want to hold educators accountable for is the speed of the movement up the ramp, not the position on the ramp."

Sanders' argument is especially popular with those who believe that urban kids from low-income backgrounds should not be constantly compared to affluent suburban students. The view has a certain common-sense logic to it — but can cut different ways. Some worry that Sanders' perspective can easily be turned into the view that "these kids aren't going to make it anyhow. Let's not expect high standards but just some growth from year to year." The fear is that some teachers, schools or policymakers will be satisfied with mere "growth" for certain groups of kids, especially low-income students of color, and therefore won't demand the resources and educational reforms necessary to ensure that all kids, regardless of background, attain high levels of achievement.

Sanders' approach has also been criticized for its methodology. Douglas Reeves, director of the Denver-based Center for Performance Assessment and an assessment consultant to MPS in the past several years, criticizes Sanders for tying conclusions about achievement to the "single instrument" of a standardized test. Reeves argues that standardized tests should be "maybe one of ten things" used to evaluate performance. Otherwise, he said, there is "the possibility of misrepresenting ... what the student really knows."

Negative Ramifications

Critics of the new MPS testing proposal fear that the advocates are too cavalier about the negative ramifications of an undue emphasis on standardized testing.

According to FairTest's Neill, "Testing all students with norm-referenced, multiple-choice tests will substantially control the curriculum and teaching," he said. "It is too high an educational price to pay for the amount of information that is gained."

Lorrie Shepard, a professor at the University of Colorado at Boulder, has argued that researchers may gain "technically sophisticated analysis," but only by "limiting the quality of the assessments used."

At a Denver conference this February, Shepard raised cautions about Sanders' value-added assessment. She noted that in Tennessee, which has been a national leader in value-added testing, "this has meant limiting assessment content to multiple-choice tests or to a commercially available test with only a limited range of test formats." Such tests, especially when used for "high-stakes" decisions, "lead to both test-score inflation and curriculum distortion," she said.

Many teachers, especially in elementary school, complain that their schools already dwell too much on the third- and fourth-grade tests. In some schools, recesses have been canceled, art and music schedules have been changed, and instruction in non-core academic areas has been curtailed

in order to provide more time for test preparation.

Removing Performance Assessments as District Mandates

A third rationale for the "Balanced Assessment System" is that performance assessments are not workable as a district wide tool.

The MPS performance assessments have their roots in the early 1990s, during adoption of the district's "K-12 Teaching and Learning Goals." At that time, "there was widespread feeling in the district at every level — principals and teachers — that the kind of testing we were doing did not represent the goals we had for kids, what we actually wanted kids to be able to do," said Hartford Principal Ellwood, then in charge of Curriculum and Instruction.

Reeves, a national expert on performance assessment, told *Rethinking Schools* "it would be a mistake" to get rid of the performance assessments as a district-wide requirement. "I am in favor of empowering schools but not empowering them to lower their expectations, which is what might happen if performance assessments become voluntary," Reeves said.

Critics argue the Milwaukee proposal will "further document failure" rather than help improve teaching and learning.

Alverno's Diez said performance assessments also do more to improve classroom learning than standardized tests, and are more classroom based. "Teachers are better able to know what the kids can do and how instruction needs to be changed to help them," she said.

The positive impact of the MPS performance assessments has been dramatic in some schools, especially in science and writing.

In some elementary schools, science instruction had consisted of reading a chapter and answering the questions at the end. With the implementation of a science performance assessment in fifth grade, elementary schools pushed a more active approach — teaching kids the scientific process, conducting experiments, and demonstrating and reflecting on their work in science fairs.

Science Scores Rise

Interestingly, science achievement scores have risen the last two years in MPS. Ellwood says she's "seen a real change in the attention to science in this district." She attributes gains to the hard work of teachers who have been pushed by the performance assessments.

AH HA! YOU DON'T FIT THE STANDARD! THAT PROVES THAT PUBLIC EDUCATION IS A FAILURE!

STANDARDIZED TESTS
THE INTELLIGENT WAY TO TEST INTELLIGENCE

KONOPACKI ©2000

HUCK/KONOPACKI LABOR CARTOONS MAY 2000 WWW.SOLIDARITY.COM/HKCARTOONS

Huck/Konopacki

"Now we are moving away from the science performance assessment, with all its flaws, and we are not going to be testing science in many of the grades throughout the district," Ellwood said. "So once again we will step away from our commitment to science."

Writing Assessment

In writing, the performance assessments pushed schools where teachers had not spent much time teaching writing or encouraging students to write. "The record clearly shows that writing assessment had an enormous impact on increasing our students' writing ability," Ellwood said. "We went from well below the national average in writing to above the national average at the elementary school [level]."

Sandra Dickerson, the MPS curriculum specialist in charge of language arts, told *Rethinking Schools* that high schools had similar positive benefits as a result of the writing proficiency and performance assessment. It had, in fact, "helped close the achievement gap between ethnic groups and helped to improve achievement across all content areas," she said.

The performance assessments are not without controversy. Their quality has varied and staff development at times has been inadequate. Some

teachers have also felt the assessments are too difficult. Despite problems, however, the performance assessments raised expectations of what students should be able to actually do, especially since they were non-negotiable and mandated by the district. "The bottom line is, teacher expectations rose because of the performance assessments," Reeves said. He also said that Milwaukee has some of the best writing achievement in the nation and that this is a direct result of the performance assessments.

Interestingly, School Board President Bruce Thompson told *Rethinking Schools* that one reason he supports the value-added standardized tests is because the performance assessments were too hard. "We make ourselves look worse because we are more demanding than other Wisconsin districts," he said. Thompson explained, for example, that in the WSAS science test "we do fairly well and then we do our own science assessment and we do miserable a year later."

Performance assessments help in the professional development of teachers in two other ways as well — through involving a group of teachers in the actual development of the prompts and by developing a core of teachers who are trained in the scoring of the assessments. These activities have proven to be positive, although the lack of

National Association for the Education of Young Children

The negative influence of standardized testing on the curriculum is not limited to kindergarten. Throughout the primary grades, schools assess achievement using tests that frequently do not reflect current theory and research about how children learn ...too many school systems teach to the test or continue to use outdated instructional methods so that children will perform adequately on standardized tests. The widespread use of standardized tests also drains resources of time and funds without clear demonstration that the investment is beneficial for children.

Ironically, the calls for excellence in education that have produced widespread reliance on standardized testing may have had the opposite effect — mediocrity. Children are being taught to provide the one "right" answer on the answer sheet, but are not being challenged to think. Rather than producing excellence, the overuse (and misuse) of standardized testing has led to the adoption of inappropriate teaching practices as well as admission and retention policies that are not in the best interest of individual children or the nation as a whole.

The ritual use even of "good tests" (those that are judged to be valid and reliable measures) is to be discouraged in the absence of documented research showing that children benefit from their use.

— From the Position Statement of the National Association for the Education of Young Children on Standardized Testing of Young Children Three Through Eight Years of Age, adopted in November 1987.

funds and some shortsightedness have led to problems. For instance, the quality of some of the assessments has been criticized. And this year, the central administration decided for financial reasons to score the performance assessments at the school level — rather than paying teachers out of central funds to meet on a citywide basis and score the assessments. In some cases, school-based scoring has lessened the consistency of the scores.

Good Reform Costs Money

Performance assessments generally cost more and require more staff development than standardized tests. One of the unanswered questions about the new testing proposal is whether it's being driven by a school board that wants to reform the district on the cheap.

"I am convinced it's a money problem," Diez told *Rethinking Schools* in answering why she thought MPS was considering the new testing proposal. "It would be too expensive to bring the system up to what it should be."

In explaining why relying on standardized testing will not improve education, Alverno's Diez offers a metaphor she learned from her father, who worked in the livestock business. "He would say, 'You don't fatten a pig by weighing it more often,'" she wrote the MPS School Board. "The kind of standardized testing being proposed in the 'Balanced Assessment System' is, in effect, simply weighing. Where are we nurturing and feeding our students so that they will be able to do well on the tests? A balanced system needs to ensure the opportunity for students to learn and grow; if it does not, then testing becomes a cruel hoax." ❑

— Bob Peterson (repmilw@aol.com) teaches fifth grade at La Escuela Fratney in Milwaukee and is an editor of Rethinking Schools. He would like to thank Larry Hoffman for research assistance.

The above is reprinted from Rethinking Schools, Vol. 14, #4, Summer 2000. The full text is available online at www.rethinkingschools.org, under "Past Issues."

A Vision of School Reform

BY THE EDITORS OF RETHINKING SCHOOLS

School reform debates are often long on rhetoric and short on substance, dominated by 30-second soundbites rather than thoughtful conversations.

As an essential starting point, discussions need to be guided by a set of principles. Developing such principles is difficult but can help create consensus, focus on priorities, reveal sometimes competing agendas, and clarify the criteria by which reforms can be judged.

Rethinking Schools offers the following working draft of a "Vision of Reform." The vision is not intended as a programmatic platform but as a set of principles that can guide the development of specific initiatives such as smaller classes or universal access to pre-kindergarten programs. The ultimate goal is to develop both principles and programs that will allow our schools to serve all students and to promote the broader social good.

Public schools are responsible to the community, not to the marketplace.

For the first time in contemporary history, the very concept of public education is at risk. This has important repercussions not only for public schools, but for the entire public sector.

Education reform must be grounded in the democratic vision that all of society is responsible for educating the next generation. Reform must be shaped by an understanding of the crucial role public schools play in helping create a multicultural democracy. That this vision has yet to be realized does not mean it should be abandoned.

Many powerful people downplay the importance of the public sector and extol marketplace approaches to school reform. Yet the market privileges individual advancement over what is best for the community. It creates profitable opportunities for private investors and encourages more privi-

leged "education consumers" to buy or move their way out of troubled schools. In the process, class and racial inequalities are exacerbated, society's collective commitment to all children is weakened, and the concept of the public good is undermined.

Schools must be actively multicultural and anti-racist, promoting social justice for all.

At a time of increasingly successful attempts to roll back the gains of the Civil Rights Movement, it is essential that schools promote an anti-racist perspective and actively combat racism. Our society and schools are shamefully stratified, and this stratification is particularly acute when it involves issues of race.

In addition to combating racism, schools must work against discrimination and prejudice in all areas. Schools must ensure that all students are full members of the school community and are not discriminated against in areas such as gender, class, sexual orientation, physical or emotional limitations, or primary use of a language other than English.

Multiculturalism, anti-racism, and social justice cannot be mere "add-ons" to a school's philosophy, culture, and curriculum. Rather, they must inform every aspect of school life — from the relations between parents, students, and staff, to the content of curriculum and teaching materials, to an all-out effort to eliminate the achievement gap between white students and students of color.

Furthermore, a multicultural, social justice perspective understands that schools must not only prepare all students to take part in society, but to transform the world they live in.

> *Reform must be shaped by an understanding of the crucial role public schools play in creating a multicultural democracy.*

The curriculum must be geared toward learning for life and the needs of a multicultural democracy.

Too often the problem is not just that students are not taught well, but they are not taught what they need to know. Curriculum reform is key to school reform.

First of all, curriculum must be based on respect for students, their innate curiosity, and their capacity to learn. It should be hopeful, joyful, kind, visionary, so students are made to feel significant and cared about — by the teacher and by each other.

A curriculum geared toward life is rooted in children's needs and experiences. It expects students to pose critical questions and to "talk back" to the world.

A democratic curriculum must be rooted in social justice, and be explicitly multicultural and anti-racist. Teachers must admit they don't "know it all" and have much to learn from their students and their students' families.

At the same time, the curriculum must be academically rigorous and teachers must set high expectations for all children. A democratic curriculum not only equips children to change the world but also to maneuver in the one that exists.

Jean-Claude Lejeune

All schools and all children must receive adequate resources.

Across the country, some children are showered with resources and attention while others are denied the bare minimum. Yet all children deserve adequate resources.

Money, well spent, matters. To cite one important example: smaller class sizes. Combined with other supports for teaching and learning, smaller class sizes can significantly improve the likelihood of higher student achievement.

It is unjust that many urban and rural districts can only spend half as much per pupil as affluent suburban districts — especially when the needs of low-income students tend to be greater.

It is also essential to recognize that distributing money equally is not automatically "fair."

Some students deserve and need extra monies, in particular low-income students who may not have as many resources in their homes and neighborhoods, students who do not speak English as their first language, and students with special educational needs.

Finally, all children deserve adequate resources from the time of their birth, so they are able to start school on an equal footing.

Reform must center on the classroom and the needs of children.

Too many educational reforms show little understanding of the day-to-day realities facing teachers and students. The reforms are top-down, bureaucratic mandates (even if couched in the rhetoric of decentralization and local control).

Rather than judging how a reform will play on the evening news, we must first ask how it will improve teaching and learning for children in the classroom. In particular, we must evaluate how a reform affects the education of low-income students and students of color.

Take, for example, the issue of "standards." Unfortunately, standards have become equated with "high-stakes" multiple choice tests that distort the curriculum, straitjacket teachers, and bully students, especially low-performing students. Instead, standards should be geared toward high-quality and rigorous academics for all children. They must be focused on improved student learning for all, not on setting up a system of rewards and punishments that legitimates existing social relations and power structures.

> *It is essential that schools promote an anti-racist perspective and actively combat racism.*

Good teachers are essential to good schools.

If we want to improve our schools, we must improve the quality of teachers, focusing on both their training in schools of education and on teachers' ongoing staff development. A commitment to quality teaching involves traditional concerns such as ensuring that teachers are certified and educated in the areas they teach, that teachers have time for ongoing professional development and discussions with colleagues, and that mentor programs be instituted for all new teachers and for veteran teachers who need help. Equally important, it means that all teachers be educated to be actively anti-racist and that teachers be expected to act on their social convictions and promote issues of social justice.

A particular focus should be on increasing the number of teachers of color and ensuring that they have access to positions of leadership. Teachers of color play a particularly important role in serving as role models, in providing valuable perspectives for all students, and in enriching discussions on how schools and teachers can set high expectations for all students and help students meet those expectations.

Reform must involve collaboration among educators, parents, and the community.

Lasting reform must be built from the ground up and must be based on mutual respect and collaboration among all those involved in public education.

Parents, in particular, have been marginalized in school reform efforts, and must be brought into the decision-making process at all levels, from the individual school to the legislative arena.

Collaboration and accountability are two-way streets. The community must provide the support and resources for schools to do their job. Schools, in turn, must understand that the community at large, not just the parents at individual schools, has the right to demand accountability from the schools.

We must revitalize our urban communities, not just our schools.

The health of our schools reflects the health of the communities they serve. Joblessness, poverty, substance abuse, and sub-standard housing undeniably affect our schools. Clearly, massive and ongoing intervention is needed to save both our urban communities and our urban schools.

Schools need the support of the broader community if they are to do their job, and schools, in turn, can help bring needed perspective and resources to solving broader social problems. Schools should serve the entire community — from the youngest toddlers to adults and the elderly — with a variety of recreational, cultural, job training, and social service programs. Such a vision is especially important for struggling neighborhoods, where schools can serve as community centers providing everything from daycare, to language classes for immigrants, to health screening, to social services such as food stamps.

Working together, schools, labor unions, community groups, religious congregations, and civic leaders can boldly address problems that are too large for any one group to solve on their own.

There is a Zulu expression: "If the future doesn't come toward you, you have to go fetch it." It is time to build a movement to go fetch a better future: in our classrooms, in our schools, and in the larger society. ❑

— *This article first appeared in Rethinking Schools, Vol. 14, #4, Summer 2000.*

FAILING OUR KIDS:
WHY THE TESTING CRAZE WON'T FIX OUR SCHOOLS

Jean-Claude Lejeune

Resources

A Glossary of Useful Terms

Standardized test

Any set of predetermined questions given to large numbers of students under the same conditions (such as a time limit) and scored in the same way. Usually refers to multiple-choice tests given statewide or nationwide. Standardized tests tend to be "norm-referenced," with the main purpose to compare and rank students.

Norm-referenced test

Tests designed to compare a student's score against the scores of a sample group called the "norming group." Most norm-referenced tests are multiple choice, although some include short-answer questions. One or two wrong answers can drastically change a score.

Bell curve

To make it easier to rank students, norm-referenced tests use a "bell curve" — in which a few test-takers score very low, a few score very high, and most are grouped in the middle. Scores are usually reported as percentile ranks, ranging from the 1st percentile to the 99th percentile. The tests are designed so that half the students will always score "below average."

Criterion-referenced test

Tests designed to evaluate whether a student has mastered certain "criteria" such as curricular objectives or areas of knowledge. Scores are reported as levels (advanced, proficient, basic, not proficient, and so forth) rather than as percentiles.

Off-the-shelf tests

National tests, almost always norm-referenced standardized tests, available from test-making companies. The most common include the Iowa Test of Basic Skills, the Stanford Achievement Test, and the CTB McGraw-Hill TerraNova.

High-stakes testing

When an educational decision is based on a single test score — whether a student will advance to the next grade level, be able to enter a preferred program or school, or even get a high school diploma. High stakes are also applied to schools and teachers, with judgment, rewards or punishments, based wholly or primarily on standardized test scores.

Performance assessments

Assessments other than multiple–choice or short–answer tests that are used to determine a student's progress toward an academic goal. The tasks are designed to evaluate performance in a real-world activity. Performance assessments include writing an essay, conducting a science experiment, giving an oral presentation, explaining in words how the student arrived at the answer to a math question, and so forth. Sometimes referred to as authentic assessments.

Portfolio assessment

Assessment based on a student's collection of work and evaluations over time. Often includes a variety of materials, from student samples, awards, drawings, audio or video tapes of student work, test scores, and teacher evaluations.

Exhibitions

Student demonstrations of a process or product which reflect what the students have learned. Exhibitions are often presented to parents and the community, providing a mechanism for school, teacher, and student acountability.

Reliability

The degree to which an assessment is able to produce consistent results over time with different groups of students or with the same students at different times. Most standardized achievement tests have fairly high reliability.

Validity

The degree to which a test actually measures what it is supposed to measure. For example, a multiple-choice test on fitness guidelines will never determine a student's physical fitness; asking a student to run, stretch, or lift weights would be a more valid measure. Multiple-choice, standardized tests tend to have high reliability but low validity.

Resources on Standards and Assessments

For a listing of additional organizations working for educational reform and justice, check out the links page at www.rethinkingschools.org.

National Organizations

Center for Law and Education. 1875 Connecticut Ave., N.W., Suite 510, Washington, DC 20009. 202-986-3000. www.cleweb.org. Involved in litigation and advocacy. Publishes a booklet for parents based on their report *Urgent Message: Families Crucial to School Reform*.

Center for Performance Assessment. 1660 S. Albion St., Suite 1002, Denver, CO 80222. 800-844-6599. users.aol.com/testdoctor. A diverse group of consultants and practitioners working with schools around the world on issues of assessment, accountability, technology, and leadership. Through their website, director Douglas Reeves, the "test doctor," responds to questions about "best practices" in these fields.

Coalition of Essential Schools. 1814 Franklin St., Suite 700, Oakland, CA 94612. 510-433-1451. www.essentialschools.org. A national network of more than 1,000 schools with a common set of principles focused on improving academic achievement by redesigning curriculum, instruction, and assessment.

FairTest. 342 Broadway, Cambridge, MA 02139. 617-864-4810. www.fairtest.org. The National Center for Fair and Open Testing (FairTest) is an advocacy organization working to end the abuses, misuses, and flaws of standardized testing and ensure that evaluation of students and workers is fair, open, and educationally sound. Quarterly newsletter (Examiner) and numerous publications. Supports local, state, and national organizing for assessment reform. See website for state contacts.

Grass Roots Innovative Policy Program (GRIPP) of the Applied Research Center. 3781 Broadway St., Oakland, CA 94611. 510-653-3415. Focuses on equity and justice in schools, hosts the ERASE program, and publishes the school report card "Making the Grade." (See p. 105.)

International Reading Association. 800 Barksdale, P.O. Box 8139, Newark, DE 18714. 302-731-1600. For their position on high-stakes testing, go to www.reading.org/advocacy/policies/high_stakes.pdf.

National Association for the Education of Young Children (NAEYC). 1509 16th St. NW, Washington, DC 20036. 800-424-2460. Leading early childhood organization that opposes the misuse of standardized testing on young children. Their position papers on testing in early childhood can be found at www.naeyc.org/about/about_index.htm.

National Center for Research on Evaluation, Standards, and Student Testing (CRESST). www.cresst96.cse.ucla.edu. Many resources including a web page devoted to resources for parents.

National Coalition of Education Activists. P.O. Box 679, Rhinebeck, NY 12572. 914-876-4580. members.aol.com/nceaweb. A network of parent, teacher, and community activists focused on organizing for equity and school reform. Many of its members work against excessive testing. Publishes the newsletter Action for Better Schools.

National Council of Teachers of English (NCTE). 1111 W. Kenyon Rd., Urbana, IL 61801. Their specific recommendations on high-stakes testing can be found at www.ncte.org/resolutions/highstakes1999.html.

National Research Council's Board on Testing and Assessment. www4.nationalacademies.org/cbsse/bota.nsf. Many reports available online, including the 1999 study High Stakes: Testing for Tracking, Promotion, and Graduation.

Rethinking Schools. 1001 E. Keefe Ave., Milwaukee, WI 53212. 800-669-4192. www.rethinkingschools.org. Publishes a quarterly news journal and books about classroom teaching and educational policy. Reports regularly on struggles against test-driven reform.

State/Local Organizations

CA-Resisters. A listserv for people interested in opting out of the California tests. To subscribe, send an email to majordomo@lists.ncte.org. In the first line of the message put: subscribe ca-resisters.

Citizens for Alternatives to Standardized Test Abuse. www.castausa.com. 316 California Ave. #9, Reno, NV 89509. castausa@hotmail.com. A group of concerned parents, students, teachers, and citizens opposed to Nevada's high-stakes proficiency tests.

Coalition for Authentic Reform in Education. www.fairtest.org/arn/masspage.html. 342 Broadway, Cambridge, MA 02139. 617-864-4810. A coalition of parents and teachers in Massachusetts opposing the MCAS and working to build support for comprehensive assessment. Contact person: Karen Hartke.

Coalition for Educational Justice. Contact: Kirti Baranwal, 939 S. St. Andrews Pl. #3, Los Angeles, CA 90019. 323-730-8570. kirtibaranwal@hotmail.com. Or contact: Ana Gallegos, 909 Ave. 52, Los Angeles, CA 90042. 323-259-9236. anag@gateway.net. A progressive, anti-racist grassroots organization of California parents and teachers. Opposes high-stakes testing and favors a broad reform program, including re-instatement of bilingual education, support for anti-racist curriculum, and a shift of state spending from prisons to schools.

Coalition for Responsible Assessment. c/o Milwaukee Catalyst, 2174 Martin Luther King Dr., Milwaukee, WI 53212. 414-264-4010. repmilw@aol.com. A coalition of community groups and individual parents and educators opposed to excessive standardized testing and in favor of alternative forms of assessment in Milwaukee.

Concerned Parents of Gwinnett. www.cpog.org. A parent group fighting the high-stakes Gateway tests in Gwinnett County, GA, as the only measure used to determine promotion of fourth and seventh graders.

Florida Coalition for Assessment Reform. www.angelfire.com/fl4/fcar. 310 Michigan Ave., Lynn Haven, FL 32444-1428. 850-265-6438. A grassroots organization providing resources and assistance to parents, teachers, students, and others who support assessment reform.

North Carolina Citizens for Democratic Schools. www.geocities.com/nccds/index.html. Contact: Irv Besecker at besecker@sprynet.com. An organization advocating community involvement in schools and an end to reliance on standardized testing as a method of evaluating students.

Parents Across Virginia United to Reform SOLs. personal.cfw.com/~dday/VASOLs.html. Contact: Mickey VanDerwerker, 506 Bedford Ave., Bedford, VA 24523. 540-586-6149. wmzemka@aol.com. PAVURSOL's goals include working to amend state law to prohibit use of SOL test scores as the primary basis for evaluating students or schools.

Parents Against TAAS Testing. www.taasblues.com. Contact: Carol M. Holst, P. O. Box 5711, Alvin, TX 77512. 281-331-9182. A way for parents to come together in opposition to the state-mandated tests in Texas.

Parents Against Unfair Proficiency Testing. www.stopOPTs.org. Contact: Mary O'Brien, 3077 Derby Road, Upper Arlington, OH 43221. 614-487-0477. A very useful website for anyone interested in fighting the Ohio Proficiency Tests.

Parents for Educational Justice. Contact: C. C. Campbell-Rock, 916 Saint Andrew St., New Orleans, LA 70131. 504-566-0032 or 504-948-6250. parentjustice@hotmail.com. A coalition of people across Louisiana demanding decent education for all children.

Parents United for Responsible Education (PURE). www.pureparents.org. 407 S. Dearborn, #515, Chicago, IL 60605. 312-461-1994. A nonprofit parent advocacy group involved in Chicago school reform. Website includes documents related to testing, particularly in Chicago.

Portland Area Rethinking Schools. Contact: Bill Bigelow at bbpdx@aol.com. A network of teachers who are active in various educational issues, including organizing against standardized testing.

Student Coalition for Alternatives to MCAS (SCAM). www.scam-mcas.org. A growing organization of Massachusetts students committed to raising awareness of the problems associated with the state's high-stakes tests — and then trying to address those problems.

Substance. 5132 W. Berteau Ave., Chicago, IL 60641-1440. 773-725-7502. Csubstance@aol.com. A monthly newspaper founded in 1975 by Chicago public school teachers to provide regular investigative and analytical reports. Extensive coverage around standards, high-stakes testing, and accountability in Chicago and nationally.

Additional Websites

Achieve. www.achieve.org. The official website of the National Education Summit, a decidedly pro-testing organization with a corporate perspective. Includes an overview of

each state's plans to "raises student performance and improve the quality of education."

Alfie Kohn. www.alfiekohn.org. Author of *The Schools Our Children Deserve* and other books, provides strategies for rescuing our students from "tougher standards" and a list of contacts in many states.

Assessment Reform Network (ARN). www.fairtest.org/arn/arn.htm. Sponsors a listserv to focus on strategies for changing assessment practices and systems in a way that is consistent with the Principles and Indicators of Student Assessment Systems of the National Forum on Assessment. (See article, p. 102)

Center for Language and Learning. www.learningrecord.org. The Learning Record is an innovative record-keeping and assessment system that focuses on student literacy performance. (See article, p. 102)

The Consortium for Equity in Standards and Testing. www.csteep.bc.edu/ctest. This website offers an abundance of links and resources.

ERIC Clearinghouse on Assessment and Evaluation. www.ericae.net. Extensive listing of resources on assessment and evaluation available on the Internet. Parent brochures available at www.accesseric.org. Covers all "sides" of testing issues.

Books and Reports — Critiques

Accountability, Assessment and Teacher Commitment: Lessons from Kentucky's Reform Efforts, ed. Betty Lou Whitford and Ken Jones (Albany, NY: State University of New York, 2000). 800-666-2211. An in-depth critique of one of the nation's most talked about reform efforts. Includes perspectives on what would constitute more authentic assessment systems.

Achievement Testing in the Early Grades: The Games Grown-Ups Play, ed. Constance Kamii (Washington, DC: National Association for the Education of Young Children, 1990). 800-424-2460. A helpful volume that both criticizes the use of standardized tests with young children and offers several assessment alternatives.

Adverse Impact! How CBEST Fails the People of California, Harold Berlak (Oakland, CA: Applied Research Center, 1999). 510-653-3415. An analysis of scientific flaws and racial bias in the test teachers must pass to get a teaching license in California.

The Bell Curve Debate: History, Documents, Opinions, ed. Russell Jacoby and Naomi Glauberman (New York: Times Books/Random House, 1995). 800-733-3000. Contains an excellent range of documents and commentaries on hereditarian interpretations of IQ tests, from their eugenic origins to the "scientific" racism of Murray and Herrnstein's *The Bell Curve* in the 1990s.

QUOTABLE QUOTE

"The problem with standardized testing is that the testing is standardized. Different learners learn differently, and different teachers teach differently, and different teacher-learner combinations work differently at different times and in different ways.

"One cannot fix such tests. Instead, one must abandon them in favor of methods of creative evaluation that are genuinely compassionate and humane and that speak to the authentic needs of teachers and students alike."

— *Richard Prystowsky, editor, Paths of Learning, and professor of English and Humanities at Irvine Valley College in California.*

PEANUTS

AN ESSAY TEST! I'M DOOMED!

WHY COULDN'T SHE HAVE GIVEN US A MULTIPLE-CHOICE TEST?

OR A TRUE OR FALSE TEST?

I HATE IT WHEN YOU HAVE TO KNOW WHAT YOU'RE WRITING ABOUT...

Schulz/United Feature Syndicate

The Big Test: A Secret History of the American Meritocracy, Nicolas Lemann (New York: Farrar, Straus and Giroux, 1999). 888-330-8477. Provides new information about the Educational Testing Service that forces us to question why we allow a private testing industry to wield such enormous influence in our public life. An important book.

The Case Against Standardized Testing: Raising the Scores, Ruining the Schools, Alfie Kohn (Westport, CT; Heinemann, 2000). 800-793-2154; An indictment of standardized testing from author and activist Alfie Kohn. A highly readable introduction to the topic.

Contradictions of School Reform: The Educational Costs of Standardized Testing, Linda McNeil (New York: Routledge, 2000). 800-634-7064. This powerful critique looks at the impact standardized testing has had on schools, teaching, and learning.

FairTest Examiner. This quarterly newsletter is the only national newsletter devoted exclusively to testing and assessment. For subscription information, contact FairTest (see above).

Inheriting Shame: The Story of Eugenics in America, Stephen Selden (New York: Teachers College Press, 1999). 800-575-6566. A must-read for educators who want to know how racist and eugenic notions of human worth became an important part of teacher training, gifted programs, and textbooks in American schools and colleges between 1910 and 1948.

The Mismeasure of Man, Stephen Jay Gould (New York: W. W. Norton, 1996, 1981). 800-233-4830. Traces the history of attempts to measure intelligence and reveals how these efforts are more successful in measuring the biases of the testers than the abilities of the tested. Provides insight into the sociopolitical context of the current push for high-stakes testing.

No Mercy: How Conservative Think Tanks and Foundations Changed America's Social Agenda, Jean Stefancic and Richard Delgado (Philadelphia: Temple University Press, 1996). 800-447-1656. An incisive analysis of the right wing's rise to power. Particularly good chapters are: "Official English;" "IQ, Race, and Eugenics;" and "The Attack on Affirmative Action."

None of the Above: The Truth Behind the SATs, Revised and Updated, David Owen and Joe Kincheloe (Lanham, MD: National Book Network, 1999). 800-462-6420. Within a broad critique of Educational Testing Service's practices and policies, this penetrating examination explodes the myth that the SATs are useful for making college admission decisions.

One Size Fits Few: The Folly of Educational Standards, Susan Ohanian (Portsmouth, NH: Heinemann, 1999). 800-225-5800.

Reading: What Can Be Measured? Second Edition, R. Farr and R. F. Carey (International Reading Association, 1986). 302-731-1600. A balanced and mainstream review of the limitations and possibilities of standardized test measures of reading.

The Schools Our Children Deserve: Moving Beyond Traditional Classrooms and "Tougher Standards," Alfie Kohn (New York: Houghton Mifflin, 1999). 800-225-3362. A well-reasoned critique of the problems with standardized tests. Includes suggestions on what schools and classrooms should be like and a one-page guide for parents on what to look for in an engaging classroom.

Shell Game: Corporate America's Agenda for Schools, Clinton Boutwell (Bloomington, IN: Phi Delta Kappa Educational Foundation, 1997). 812-339-1156. A progressive critique of the corporate role in the standards movement.

Standardized Minds: The High Price of America's Testing Culture and What We Can Do to Change It, Peter Sacks (New York Perseus Books, 1999). 800-386-5656. An excellent, refreshing critique. Places America's testing obsession within a political and historical context. Includes profiles of schools and families that have suffered under the "one-size-fits-all" mentality of high-stakes testing.

Standardized Tests and Our Children: A Guide to Testing Reform, FairTest (Cambridge, MA: FairTest, 1991). 617-864-4810. An easy-to-read guide to testing for parents, teachers, administrators, and activists. Addresses problems and misuses of standardized tests, defines terms, outlines parents' rights, and gives tips for organizing. English and Spanish versions and a NY state edition are available.

A Teacher's Guide to Standardized Reading Tests: Knowledge Is Power, Lucy Calkins, Kate Montgomery, and Donna Santman (Portsmouth, NH: Heinemann, 1998). 800-225-5800.

Testing Our Children: A Report Card on State Assessment Systems, Monty Neill (Cambridge, MA: FairTest, 1997). 617-864-4810. An overview of the testing craze throughout the United States.

Will Standards Save Public Education? ed. Deborah Meier (Boston: Beacon Press, 2000). 800-225-3362. This short book examines the relationship between schooling, standards, and democracy. Includes essays by Bob Chase, Gary Nash, Theodore Sizer, Bill Ayers, and others.

Books and Reports — Alternative Assessments

The American Literacy Profile Scales: A Framework for Authentic Assessment, Patrick Griffin, Patricia Smith, and Lois Burrill (Portsmouth, NH: Heinemann, 1995). 800-225-5800. An excellent approach to assessing reading, writing, speaking, and listening based on teacher observation of what students do.

Authentic Assessment in Action: Studies of Schools and Students at Work, Linda Darling-Hammond, J. Ancess, and B. Falk, (New York: Teacher College Press, 1995). A powerful set of case studies on the development of performance assessments and their positive effects on schools. Includes chapters on the use of portfolios at Central Park East Secondary School and the use of the Primary Language Record at P.S. 261.

Changing the View: Student-Led Parent Conferences, Terri Austin (Portsmouth, NH: Heinemann, 1994). 800-225-5800. A teacher-friendly guide to implementing student-led conferences in elementary through high school.

Great Performances: Creating Classroom-Based Assessment Tasks, Larry Lewin and Betty Jean Shoemaker (Alexandria, VA: Association for Supervision and Curriculum Development, 1998). 800-933-2723. A guide to developing and using a variety of performance tasks in the classroom. Includes rubrics and sample tasks.

A Guide to Authentic Instruction and Assessment: Vision, Standards and Scoring, Fred Newmann, Walter Secada, and Gary Wehlage (Madison, WI: University of Wisconsin, 1995). 800-621-2736. This guide lays out specific standards consistent with a vision of human achievement distinct from conventional school achievement.

Implementing Performance Assessments: A Guide to Classroom, School and System Reform, Monty Neill et al. (Cambridge, MA: FairTest, 1996). 617-864-4810. Provides teachers, administrators, and parents with a comprehensive look at performance assessments in the classroom and systemwide.

Multiple Intelligences: The Theory in Practice, Howard Gardner (New York: Basic Books, 1993). 800-386-5656. Examines the ways in which narrow definitions of intelligence are inadequate.

The Portfolio Organizer: Succeeding with Portfolios in Your Classroom, C. Rolheiser, B. Bower, and L. Stevahn (Alexandria, VA: ASCD, 2000). 800-933-2723. A comprehensive, teacher-friendly guide to portfolios.

Responsive Evaluation: Making Valid Judgments About Student Literacy, ed. Brian Cambourne and Jan Turbill (Portsmouth, NH: Heinemann, 1994). 800-225-5800. A detailed description of how a group of educators developed an authentic assessment system of children's literacy.

Using the Primary Language Record, M. Barrs et al. (Portsmouth, NH: Heinemann, 1988). 800-225-5800. An excellent, succinct explanation of how and why children acquire literacy and how to document and assess their literacy behaviors. Developed for use with multilingual school populations. For primary and elementary grades.

The Whole Language Evaluation Book, K. S. Goodman, Y. Goodman, and W. Hood (Portsmouth, NH: Heinemann, 1988). 800-225-5800. An excellent anthology, written from a classroom perspective, on how to implement holistic forms of assessment in classrooms from kindergarten to 12th grade.

The Work Sampling System, S. J. Meisels (Ann Arbor: Rebus Planning Associates, 1992). 800-435-3085. A specific, well-respected portfolio system for elementary schools.

"RETHINKING SCHOOLS

offers some of the freshest, most authentic insights into schools, teaching, and students' lives of any publication available. I read it because it tells it like it is"

Linda Darling-Hammond
professor of teaching and
teacher education
Stanford University

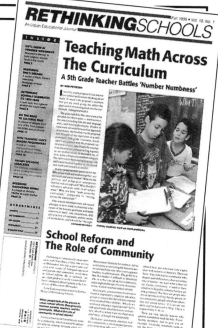

Rethinking Schools is an independent, quarterly journal committed to equity and social justice. It is written by teachers, parents, and educational activists — people who understand the day-to-day realities of reforming our schools. It asks questions, but also looks for answers. It is grounded in classroom practice, but also analyzes broader policy issues.

Rethinking Schools has one overriding concern: to help transform our schools so they can provide a quality education for all children. Every issue includes:

- Articles on how to improve classroom teaching

- Listings of valuable resources

- Analyses of complex issues like the charter school movement or curriculum standards.

Subscribe today and receive the leading grassroots voice for school reform.

Subscription rates:
$25 Two-year subscription (Save $5.00)
$15 One-year subscription
$4 Sample copy

Four Easy Ways to Subscribe!
Secure online ordering: www.rethinkingschools.org
Call toll-free: 1-800-669-4192   9am - 5pm (Central Time)
Mail order to: Rethinking Schools, 1001 E. Keefe Ave., Milwaukee, WI 53212
Fax order to: 414-964-7220

Visa, MasterCard and purchase orders accepted.

Special bulk subscription rates are available to current subscribers at greatly reduced rates — ideal for schools of education, unions, parent groups, and classroom teachers! Contact our office for details.

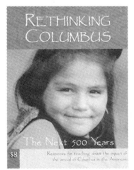

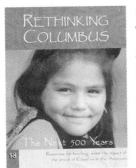

FAILING OUR KIDS:
Why the Testing Craze Won't Fix Our Schools

Edited by Kathy Swope and Barbara Miner

Whether you're a parent, teacher, student, or policymaker, it's impossible to ignore how the long arm of standardized testing is reaching into every nook and cranny of education. Yet relying on standardized tests distorts student learning, exacerbates inequities for low-income students and students of color, and undermines true accountability.

Failing Our Kids includes more than 50 articles that provide a compelling critique of standardized tests and also outline alternative ways to assess how well our children are learning.

Paperback • 148 pp. • ISBN 0-942961-26-9

Only $8 each!
Two for $12!

Special bulk rates
2 - 10 copies $6/each
11 -24 copies $5/each
25+ copies $4/each
Over 100 copies, call our office

Plus shipping and handling
U.S. shipping and handling costs are 10% of the total. Minimum s&h charge of $3.50.

Canadian shipping and handling costs are $25% of the total. Minimum s&h charge of $4.50.

"Failing Our Kids is informative, thoughtful, and compassionate. The book is part fact sheet, part clear-eyed analysis, and part passionate cry for our children's future."

— William Ayers is a distinguished professor of education at the University of Chicago, Illinois. His most recent book is *A Kind and Just Parent*.

CALL TOLL-FREE: 1-800-669-4192
ORDER ONLINE AT www.rethinkingschools.org
MASTERCARD, VISA, AND PURCHASE ORDERS ACCEPTED.

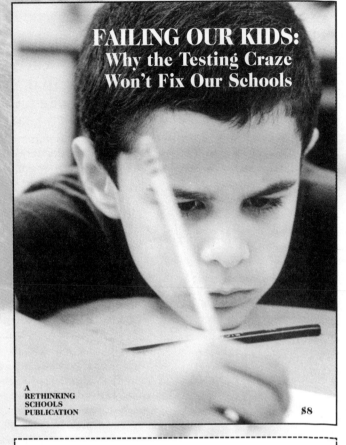

FAILING OUR KIDS:
Why the Testing Craze
Won't Fix Our Schools

A RETHINKING SCHOOLS PUBLICATION

$8

Order Form

Name _____

Org._____

Address _____

City/State/Zip _____

Phone _____

E-mail_____

___Number of copies x $_____(Unit Price) =

Subtotal $ _____

+ Shipping and Handling $ _____

Total $ _____

Method of Payment

[ ] Check or Money Order made out to
     Rethinking Schools
[ ] Purchase Order
[ ] MasterCard   [ ] Visa

Credit Card No. _____

Exp. Date_____

Authorized Signature _____

Mail to:
RETHINKING SCHOOLS
1001 E. Keefe Ave., Milwaukee, WI 53212
Fax: 414-964-7220 • Toll-free: 1-800-669-4192

CALL 1-800-669-4192 FOR A FREE CATALOG OF ALL OUR MATERIALS.